D1642417

DEATH OF A CIRCUIT

Being Some Account of

The Oxford Circuit

and

How It Was Abolished

by

GRAEME WILLIAMS

Queen's Counsel, Bencher of the Inner Temple,
sometime a Crown Court Recorder, and sometime a
member successively of the Oxford, and of the
Midland & Oxford Circuits, and a present
member of the Midland Circuit.

Wildy, Simmonds & Hill Publishing

Death of a Circuit: Being Some Account of The Oxford Circuit
and How it was Abolished

Copyright © 2006 Graeme Williams

British Library Cataloguing-in-Publication Data:
A catalogue record for this book is available from The British
Library

ISBN 1 898029 86 5

First published in 2006 by

Wildy, Simmonds & Hill Publishing
58 Carey Street, London WC2A 2JB
England

This is a story that needed to be told and Graeme Williams QC is to be congratulated on telling it. If he had not done so the contribution that the Oxford Circuit has made to the English and Welsh legal system could have been lost to future generations of lawyers, and those many non-lawyers who find legal reminiscences irresistible. In addition, a rich store of anecdotes about a wide spectrum of advocates, who in their day dominated the courts on the Circuit, would have been forgotten for ever.

It is easy to underestimate the contribution that the Oxford Circuit made to our legal system. It was after all only one of the seven circuits that had existed for over 800 years. However each of those circuits, in addition to ensuring that the same quality of justice reached every corner of England and Wales, also acted as the nursery in which the majority of young barristers learnt their trade and built up a practice. "Learning their trade" included learning the standards of conduct that are at least as important today as they ever were. They included complete integrity, never taking an unfair advantage of a colleague, never misleading the court, always preparing your case meticulously and, when necessary, ensuring that so far as possible justice was done to your client whatever the odds against him.

On all the circuits the standards of conduct required of their members was extremely high. Each circuit was jealous of its standards and they were vigorously enforced by the peer pressure that was possible because of the limited size and intimacy of each of the circuits. No two circuits were precisely the same. Each circuit had somewhat different practices from the others. Their richness depended upon the sum of their parts.

Certainly, based on my own experience, as one of the dying breed who can still claim with considerable pride that he learnt his trade on the Oxford Circuit, I can confirm that the Circuit was a demanding task master. It required many hours of travel, late nights and early mornings. However, at the same time it was a wonderful source of great companionship and deep friendships. It was a world where, once you were a member of the Circuit, your background before you became a member was irrelevant. Every member was equal; though that did not mean the junior members should not treat their more senior colleagues with appropriate respect. While the new member and the most senior member of the Circuit were equal, the more senior had the infinite advantage of being vastly experienced.

In a profession, where the real training took place on your feet when appearing as an advocate, the fact that a senior advocate was never so busy that he was unable to help a more junior colleague with sage advice was a huge advantage. I would be surprised if there is any barrister or former barrister of the Circuit, who could not still remember the unstinting help he received from his senior brothers in the law.

This generosity is only one reason why I am so pleased that, despite his health problems, Graeme Williams has managed to write this book. It is now 35 years since the Circuit was dismembered. It is simple to do the arithmetic that means there are a rapidly diminishing number of Oxford Circuiteers still alive today, who are capable of recalling the valuable material needed to enable the contemporary reader to understand and enjoy the life on the Oxford Circuit before it became no more.

Thanks to Graeme we, and our successors, will be able to relive those days which in retrospect appear so fascinating. In the life of the law 35 years is virtually a moment, but the scale of the changes that have taken place in the intervening years is extraordinary as this book makes clear. From this book the reader will be reminded, or learn, of a more leisurely, less commercial world. A world which was gentlemanly; a world where earnings did not play quite the dominant role they do today. It was a world in which it was possible to practice a profession adopting only the highest standards. They are standards which of necessity had to change to accommodate the harsher, highly competitive contemporary life of the barrister today. Yet it is a world which it would be unwise to regard as being of only historical interest. It was a world where integrity was critical, and the integrity of the barrister is still critical today.

Present and future generations will be able to learn of the spirit of those times. Today the practices before 1972 may appear to belong more to the Victorian times than today, but this does not detract from the charm and glamour of the world this book describes so well. They are times which I look back on with great affection, knowing that despite the changes that have taken place since, they provide part of the explanation why still the career of a barrister can provide more satisfaction than any other.

However there is yet one more reason why I regard this book as being important. It is that what happened to the Oxford Circuit has a lesson not only for us today, but for future generations as well. The lesson being that if you prize an institution of which you are part, even a modest part, you have to be prepared to fight for its continued existence. Fight for it, not to protect it from necessary reform, but fight for it to avoid it being unjustifiably damaged or destroyed.

The Oxford Circuit was an ancient and venerable part of our legal establishment, which had served our legal system well over hundreds of years. Sadly, it was allowed to die because a generation of members of which Graeme and I were but two relatively junior members, were all too conscious of its shortcomings for what lay ahead, and, being dispirited by this, failed to do what was needed to restore its vigour before it was too late. At least in part, as this book describes, as a result the Oxford Circuit was consigned to a lingering death by a report that did not even mention why this action was necessary.

ACKNOWLEDGEMENTS

I wish to express my thanks to all those who have helped me to write this book. In particular I am grateful to Margaret Clay, the Librarian of the Inner Temple, and her staff, to the staff of the Bodleian Library, of the British Library and of the National Archives, and to former Oxford circuiteers too numerous to mention individually. But the following have made contributions and corrections which must be, and are, gratefully acknowledged: (alphabetically), Rt. Hon. Sir Stephen Brown, H.H. Peter Crawford Q.C., Sir Michael Davies (sadly, very recently deceased), Mr Alexander Dawson, H.H. Alan King-Hamilton Q.C., Sir Oliver Popplewell, H.H. Harold Wilson A.E., and Rt. Hon. Lord Woolf, who has also most kindly written a Foreword.

In addition I would like to thank Karen Murphy who has patiently typed, and retyped, the manuscript, Vicky Wharton who designed the book's cover, Jemima Stratford who suggested my publishers to me, Dr Brian Hill of Wildy, Simmonds & Hill, the most easy-going of publishers, Valerie Roach, who gave me encouragement when I needed it, but most of all my dear wife Anna, who has put up with my filing system (numerous shopping baskets) all over our house for the last year and who, despite being a Northern circuiteer, has made many very helpful suggestions, when I needed them. To her, and to the rest of my family (daughters, sons-in-law and grandchildren) this book is very affectionately dedicated.

G.W.

CONTENTS

		Page
Foreword (by Rt. Hon. Lord Woolf)		iii
Acknowledgements.		vii
Table of Cases		xi
Table of Illustrations		xii
Table of Statutes		xiii
Bibliography		xiv
Introduction		1
Chapter 1	How it was	3
Chapter 2	What went wrong	15
Chapter 3	The Doctor's Remedy	25
Chapter 4	Taking the Medicine (in Three Gulps)	35
Chapter 5	What we have lost	46
Chapter 6	Lord Campbell's insult refuted	58
Chapter 7	How it is	66
Appendix I	The old Circuit system, and the Oxford/Midland disputes	77
Appendix II	The Reading Juke-Box Case	84
Index		93

Table of Cases

Bardell v Pickwick (unreported)	78
Haley v London Electricity Board [1965] A.C. 778	50
R. v. Herbert Rowse Armstrong (unreported) (1922) Hereford Assizes	59
R. v. John Foster, ex parte the Oxford Circuit (unreported)	50
R. v. Howard Gray (1900) 82 L.T. 534	59
R. v. Michael Chetwynd Talbot, ex parte the Oxford Circuit (unreported) (1955)	50
R. v. Edward Terrell, ex parte the Oxford Circuit (unreported) (1954)	49

Table of Illustrations

J.Andrews' map of the English and Welsh Circuits   13
(by courtesy of The Inner Temple)

Lord Beeching, looking self-satisified   24
(by courtesy of the National Portrait Gallery)

Brian Gibbens QC, trying not to laugh   40
(by courtesy of Oxford Crown Court)

Portrait of HH Judge Mynett QC,
in Court 1 in St Aldates'   41
(photograph by the author)

Oxford Assize Court   54
(photograph by the author)

Memorial outside Oxford Assize Court   54
(photograph by the author)

HH Judge Stephen Tumim, looking relaxed   61
(by courtesy of Lady Tumim)

HH Judge James Irvine, looking friendly   63
(by courtesy of Oxford Crown Court)

Note from HH Judge Claude Duveen QC
to Mr David Ashton   65
(by courtesy of Mr David Ashton)

HH Judge Peter Crawford QC, looking pleased   81
(by courtesy of Oxford Crown Court)

HH Judge King-Hamilton QC, looking percipient   82
(by courtesy of himself)

HH Judge John Murchie, thinking of a rhyme   87
(by courtesy of Mrs.John Murchie and
Messrs Ede & Ravenscroft)

TABLE OF STATUTES

Central Criminal Court Act 1834	17
Courts Act 1971	36
Criminal Evidence Act 1898	20
Criminal Justice Administration Act 1956	17
False Personation Act 1874	50
Magna Carta 1215	4
Night Poaching Act 1844	50
Steam Whistles Act 1872	49
Supreme Court Act 1981	36
Supreme Court of Judicature (Consolidation) Act 1925	37

BIBLIOGRAPHY

Anonymous *Silence in Court*, London, 2004

Atlay, J.B. *The Victorian Chancellors,* 2 Vols, London, 1908

Bellot, Hugh H.L. M.A. D.C.L. *The Temple*, London, 1914

Bosanquet, Sir Ronald QC *The Oxford Circuit,* London, 1951

Campbell, Lord(John) *Life,* 2 Vols, London 1881

Darling, Sir Charles *On the Oxford Circuit,* London, 1904/1924

Heuston, F.R.V. *Lives of the Lord Chancellors 1940-1970*, Oxford, 1987.

MacKinnon, Sir Frank Douglas *On Circuit 1924-1937*, Cambridge U.P., 1941

Megarry, R.E.,QC *Miscellany-at-Law,* London, 1955.

Nield, Sir Basil *Farewell to the Assizes,* London, 1972.

Pevsner, Prof. Nikolaus *The Buildings of England*, Leicstershire, London, 1980.

Potter, Beatrix *The Tale of Mr Tod,* London,1912.

Various Authors *The Oxford Dictionary of National Biography*, 2004

INTRODUCTION

The City of Oxford's name is attached to a surprisingly various range of phenomena: an affected English accent, a religious Movement, a cut of trousers, a Haydn symphony, kinds of marmalade and pillow cases, a street and a circus in London, a road and a railway station in Manchester, some nineteen towns in the USA, a tiny village in Barbados, (of course) numerous dictionaries and works of reference and ... a university, or two. This book is concerned with a legal Circuit which also bore Oxford's name, and with how it came to be abolished.

There are many other former Oxford circuiteers (and there *were* many more) better qualified than I am to write this book. As the years since the passing of the Courts Act 1971 have themselves passed, and those who should have written it have either shown no inclination to write it, or died, I have come reluctantly to the conclusion that, if it is to be done at all, I had better do it myself, and quickly – particularly as I have recently survived three potentially fatal illnesses. I am one of the very few remaining Oxford circuiteers still (just) in practice, though many others survive on the Bench or in retirement. I intend to send an early draft of the book to some of these, inviting their corrections, additions or subtractions.

Another consideration has emboldened me to write the book. I was really startled to find in the late 1980's whilst we were driving to Court together, that a junior member of my chambers, whom I was leading, knew virtually nothing of the former Court system which had been abolished only about 15 years before. The Beeching Report (which led to the Courts Act 1971) recommended the abolition of not only the Oxford Circuit – covertly, as will be recounted below – but also, overtly, the ancient and historic Courts system of Assizes and Quarter Sessions, which it had been appointed to consider, and on which I practised from 1960 onwards. It follows that at the time of writing a lawyer must be about 60 to have *any* personal professional experience of the system before the Act of 1971. Law students have had since 1971 quite enough to learn without bothering to understand what the criminal legal system *was*. So even middle-aged solicitors, barristers and judges have every reason to be wholly ignorant of how things went on before 1972, much as my generation were and are of civil procedure before the radical reforms of the 1870s.

I believe that some account of both the demise of the Oxford Circuit and of the previous criminal Court system may be of interest to present and possibly future practitioners, and to even a wider public. At least the information ought to be available *somewhere*, in (I hope) a more accessible form than the Parliamentary Papers referred to in Chapters 2 & 3.

I must make it clear at the outset that I have not attempted to write the modern history of the Oxford Circuit as a whole. I have confined myself to what I can claim to know about at first hand, that is, the London end of the Circuit, mostly Berkshire and Oxfordshire, but not the Birmingham or the Western areas where I ventured only rarely during my years of Circuit practice, from 1960 to the early 1980s.

In 1951 His Honour Sir Ronald Bosanquet KC, a retired Official Referee, published a rather boring but quite informative account of the Circuit in his day. It is not very enterprisingly entitled *The Oxford Circuit*. However it contains an interesting penultimate chapter about the notorious Armstrong poisoning case, tried at Hereford Assizes before the infamous Darling J., who appears again in Chapter 6 below. Sir Ronald's book and mine overlap at a very few points.

The truth is that I have enjoyed writing this book enormously.

GRAEME WILLIAMS
13, King's Bench Walk,
Inner Temple, EC4.
September 2006

CHAPTER 1

How it was

Readers of Beatrix Potter's masterpiece, *The Tale of Mr. Tod*, will recall the climactic scene (brilliantly illustrated by the author), where Mr. Tod breaks into his own house, believing that the trespassing Tommy Brock is there, in his (Mr. Tod's) bed, and finds:

> *"Tommy Brock ... sitting at Mr. Tod's kitchen table, pouring out tea from Mr. Tod's tea-pot into Mr. Tod's tea-cup ... and he threw the cup of scalding tea all over Mr. Tod".*

A violent fight ensued.

I felt much as Mr. Tod must have felt, when I saw John Cleese, in the climactic scene of that other more recent masterpiece *A Fish called Wanda*, playing a barrister and standing in my place in Oxford Town Hall's Court, where I had regularly practised at the Oxford City Quarter Sessions. He was wearing robes identical to those I used to wear, addressing a judge who looked remarkably like the Recorder of Oxford. Luckily for me, Mr. Cleese did not have the chance to throw anything at or over me, though he might well have done, granted the agitated state he seemed to be in; but a violent fight ensued there too.

This book is about how this happened, how Oxford Town Hall's Court dropped out of its intended use and became a film set, and how the system and the circuit of which it was a part were abolished. I believe this sad story has not been told in detail before. To understand it, it is necessary also to understand, at least in outline, what the system was before 1st January 1972. Readers who were in practice in circuit crime before that date can skip the rest of this chapter.

Until 1972, the system of trial and disposal of criminal cases in England and Wales had changed remarkably little for very many years, even centuries, despite some abortive mid-Victorian and later attempts at reform. In brief the system was as follows.

Every criminal case began, then as now, in a magistrates' court. The magistrates were mostly laymen (and latterly women), advised by a legally qualified clerk. In the big cities there were also a few full-time professionally qualified magistrates, then called stipendiaries. The vast majority of cases, were dealt with once and for all, then as now, in the magistrates' courts. The more serious cases were committed for trial (by jury, if the accused pleaded not guilty) to either the Assizes or Quarter Sessions, depending on the gravity of the charge.

Assizes

The judges of the Assizes were High Court Judges of the Queen's Bench, or of the Probate, Divorce and Admiralty Divisions of the High Court, or very senior barristers in line for appointment to the High Court Bench. Judges of the Chancery Division, with rare and often disastrous exceptions, did not preside at Assizes. The Assizes heard the most serious criminal cases: homicide, rape, robbery, very serious assaults, frauds and the like, and also, if time permitted (as it often did not), civil cases arising locally.

The Assize judges, and their retinue of clerks, marshals (young barristers, learning the job), and servants (including a cook and a butler), were the direct lineal successors of a system established in England in the Middle Ages. Some say it began in the reign of King Edward I in the late 13th century; others trace it to Magna Carta in 1215. Some clear indication of the antiquity of the practice of judges going on circuit is given by quotations dating from 1494 and 1503 supporting the written use of the word 'cyrcuyte' in this sense in the *Oxford English Dictionary*.[1]

---

1 'Iudgys ordeyned to kepe a cyrcuyte, as nowe they kepe the sysys in the tyme of vacacyon': Robert Fabyan, The Newe cronycles of Englande and of Fraunce. 'The justices of assizes in ther cyrcuyte or progresse in that shyre':

Even earlier, Geoffrey Chaucer, writing in the 1380's, says of the Serjeant-at-Law (one of the Canterbury Pilgrims), 'Justice he was ful often in assise, By patent, and by pleyn commissioun'.

The Sovereign's judges were sent out from London two or three times a year to travel the length and breadth of the country, sitting in Court to hear and determine ('oyer et terminer', in law French) the serious criminal cases, in each *county*, usually in the county town. They resided there, in lodgings which it was the duty of the sheriff of the county, or other local authorities, to provide. A picturesque and archaic feature of the Assizes was the huge wicker hamper, of the size and type in which Sir John Falstaff so unwisely took refuge in Ford's house.[2] In this the Court's books, papers and other impedimenta were carried from one Assize town to the next.

Each Circuit had a permanent staff, headed by the Clerk of Assize (a powerful official) with several subordinates. They travelled from town to town with the Judge – and the hamper. In my day the Oxford Circuit's Clerk of Assize was a genial Welshman named Bill Lewis T.D. He had been in practice on the Oxford Circuit before the War, and thereafter (on health grounds) had worked in the office of the Director of Public Prosecutions, before taking the job on the Circuit, where he was a very popular figure.

The way of life of a judge of Assize in the 1920s and '30s is admirably depicted in Sir Frank MacKinnon's book entitled *On Circuit*, written and published during the early 1940s, after his promotion to the Court of Appeal. It is an entertaining and learned work, full of recondite information: I have drawn on it quite substantially in what follows. MacKinnon J. frequently had only one or two cases (criminal or civil) to try, sometimes none at all, at towns such as Bedford in 1929 or Oxford in 1932.[3]

Statute 9 Henry VII cap 7. *OED* 2nd ed Vol III p. 229..

2   see *Merry Wives of Windsor*, Act III Scene 3 and Verdi, Act II Scene 2.

3   see MacKinnon op. cit. pp.159 & 218 and generally p.188.

The judges' travels were organised in a series of groups of counties adjacent to each other. These groups may well be the origins of the Circuits. According to MacKinnon[4] the first grouping was into four unnamed 'Circuits' in the 13th century. The counties which were later to be included in the Oxford Circuit were allotted to two groups, roughly corresponding to the present Midland and Western Circuits.

The Assize system had many defects, as will appear in the next chapter. But it had the great merit of encouraging uniformity of Court procedure across the country and also some supervision by the visiting Judges of local Court practice, and malpractice.

Quarter Sessions

The Courts of Quarter Sessions heard the middle-ranking criminal cases – burglaries, thefts, less serious assaults, affrays, many motoring offences, and appeals from the Magistrates' Courts. The system, no doubt deriving from obscure medieval origins, was complicated, illogical and inconvenient. The first recorded written use of the term is in 1577.[5]

There were two kinds of Quarter Sessions Courts, with almost identical jurisdiction: County Quarter Sessions, and City and Borough Quarter Sessions.

Every county and all the Cities, and many, but not all, *Boroughs* had Courts of Quarter Sessions. I do not know, and for present purposes it does not matter, how this happened. The judge of the City or Borough Quarter Sessions (hereafter treated as one) was the Recorder, who was a practising barrister, usually, but not always, a Queen's Counsel (QC). He (or, rarely, she) was the Recorder of *that* Borough, and sat in that capacity only there, unlike the post-1971 Recorders who can sit in the Crown Court anywhere they are asked to. If the work to be done at Borough

---

4   op. cit. page 115

5   see O.E.D.Vol. XII page 988.

Quarter Sessions was more than the Recorder could cope with, a mid-Victorian Act enabled him to appoint a deputy to sit either at the same time as, or at other times than, himself. Appointment as Recorder, particularly of the large towns and cities, was a professionally honorific matter for its recipient, and possibly a harbinger of further promotion in the future. On the Oxford Circuit there were nineteen Boroughs with their own Quarter Sessions, and hence nineteen Recorderships. No other Circuit had more, and only the South-Eastern had as many.

County Quarter Sessions had the same jurisdiction as Borough Quarter Sessions, but their judges were a curious assortment ranging, in 1969, from 146 practising barristers to 2 professors of law, 2 solicitors, and 1 retired Lord Chancellor. Each County Sessions had a Chairman and number of *permanent* (but part-time) Deputy Chairmen. In about half the counties the Chairman was a practising barrister, and again it was an honorific appointment. Appointment as a Deputy Chairman was, however, not only a professional, but in some posh counties also a social, accolade. On the Oxford Circuit, appointment as a Deputy Chairman of the Salop County Sessions was sought by, but not granted to, persons not regarded as socially worthy by the ancient Chetwynd Talbot family. In the 1960s one of its members, the delightfully loquacious Michael, was the Chairman. He dropped the first of his two surnames whilst at the Bar, but picked it up again when he became a Circuit judge under the new regime.

Another curious feature of the County Quarter Sessions was that the Chairman and his Deputies, if not barristers in practice, were in many cases also full-time judges elsewhere[6]. So Oxon Quarter Sessions had in 1970 Sir Edward Eveleigh (a High Court Judge) as Chairman, and His Honour Judge Alan King-Hamilton QC (an Old Bailey Judge) as one of its Deputy Chairmen, the

---

6   This happened because, if a barrister was appointed as a chairman or deputy chairman, and later accepted a full-time judicial appointment, he could, if he wished (as most did), retain the job at Quarter Sessions. A Recorder, on the other hand, had to resign.

latter a former leader of the Oxford Circuit, and still very much alive at the age of 101. These judges, if they wished to maintain their circuit connections, could sit at Quarter Sessions only when their other judicial duties allowed: i.e. in the High Court or Old Bailey vacations or recesses. Before New Year's Day became a public holiday, Oxon Quarter Sessions could, and often did, sit on 1st January. I once drove through the night from a family New Year's Eve party in Anglesey to appear at Oxon Sessions at 10 am on 1st January. It also meant that the various County Sessions tended to sit at the same time as each other, and also at the same time as the Recorders of the City and Borough Sessions.

Some of the barrister judges of Quarter Sessions were pluralists. Robert Hutton (a very senior and respected junior: i.e. non-QC) was both the Recorder of Reading and the Chairman of Gloucestershire Quarter Sessions, and Brian Gibbens QC was both the Recorder of Oxford and a deputy Chairman of Oxon Quarter Sessions. He seldom sat in the latter capacity, because there was more than enough work for him in the former, quite apart from his busy practice at the Bar.[7]

A vestigial feature of Trollopian England was the entitlement of lay county magistrates to sit at the county Sessions, with a legally qualified chairman or deputy. Within living memory (not mine!) Lord Macclesfield, a bluff, jovial aristocrat without legal qualification, used to *preside* at Oxon Quarter Sessions, sometimes with his son, also a lay magistrate, beside him. However, by the 1960s, the lay magistrates' function there was far from clear. They obviously enjoyed hobnobbing with the lawyers, especially the judges, and with Lord Macclesfield. But when the serious business of trying criminals began, most of them tended to disappear back to their rural estates.

The Recorders and their Deputies at the Borough Sessions sat in Court wearing their professional robes. But the Chairmen and their Deputies at the County Sessions sat in mufti. It ought

---

7   see pages 19-20 below.

perhaps to be recorded here (if nowhere else, though I never witnessed it) that at Wiltshire County Sessions, at Devizes on the Western Circuit, the Chairmen and Deputies sat (all day) wearing black silk top hats, with their dark suits.

For no reason that I know of, the lay magistrates of a borough either did not have, or chose not to exercise, a right to sit in Court with the Recorder. However when I was an undergraduate reading law at Oxford, one of my tutors was an Oxford City magistrate (and a non-practising barrister). I have a distinct, but possibly mistaken, recollection of seeing him watching me in action in the Oxford Town Hall Court. He was wearing the same familiar, pained expression which I remembered then, and remember now, in reaction to my advocacy, as he had worn while listening to me reading an essay on Trusts for Sale, a few years earlier.

Both Borough and County Quarter Sessions were staffed by employees of the Borough or the County respectively, who (at least in theory) had other jobs as well. The Town Clerk of the City of Oxford, an important local government post, was also *ex officio* the Clerk of the Peace of the City Quarter Sessions, that is the Court's clerk and chief official. In the early 1960s he used to sit in Court, at least on the first day of each sitting, when the Recorder also sat to deal with the cases in which the accused were known to be going to plead guilty. Similarly, at the Oxon County Sessions, both the Clerk of the Peace and his Deputy had other posts in the County's employ, the latter as the County Archivist.

No doubt 'originally' Quarter Sessions sat once a quarter. But by the 1960s both the Borough and the County Sessions were, even in the smaller towns such as Abingdon and Banbury, sitting much more frequently. They also often coincided with the Assizes[8] in a nearby county on the circuit. There was no overall

---

8 This was not a new problem. J.B. Atlay, in Vol. 2 of The Victorian Chancellors, page 142, writing in 1908, recalled that 'Reading and Oxford (Assizes) ... clashed with the London sitting ...' in the 1820's. Until the revolutionary legislation of 1873, the Circuit sittings usually took place in the

control of when the various courts sat. Each borough and county was autonomous, and was also independent of the arrangements for Assizes. On the Oxford Circuit, the Quarter Sessions in five Black Country Boroughs (Wolverhampton, Walsall etc) operated a successful system in the 1960s to avoid clashes between them. But it was becoming a national problem and, as events proved, local solutions were not enough. The inexorable growth in Court business began to take over the working days of the employees of the Boroughs and the Counties; their part-time Court jobs became almost full-time, and new, inexperienced assistants were hastily recruited, sometimes with regrettable results.

On many Circuits, barristers had to join (and pay for doing so) 'the Bar Mess' for particular Quarter Sessions. On the Oxford Circuit all the Quarter Sessions were 'open' to all members of the Circuit.

The Bar and the Circuits

In order to provide advocacy at Assizes and Quarter Sessions, the Bar divided itself into Circuits, reflecting the Circuits of the Assize judges. With a few far-flung exceptions in Cornwall and Lincolnshire, the Bar had exclusive rights of audience at both Assizes and Quarter Sessions. During the 1960s solicitors were constantly challenging these rights, without much if any success. At the same time their own more remunerative monopoly in conveyancing was being successfully eroded by 'licensed conveyancers'. The Bar felt the solicitors would have done better looking after their own work rather than trying to get ours.

For very many years, practising barristers have also grouped themselves into sets of chambers: a commercially unusual arrangement in which the members share expenses (rent, staff salaries, and the like), but *not* incomes, and are *not* partners. It follows that it is possible, and in fact very common, for members

---

vacations of the Courts in London: a change which Atlay, op.cit. Vol 2 page 418 described as 'killing the circuits'; but most of them seem to have survived...

of the same set of chambers to be on opposing sides in the same case. This would present serious problems if ever partnerships were introduced at the Bar. In my professional life-time (1960 to date) the role played in a barrister's life by his (or increasingly her) chambers, and the character of a set of chambers, have changed almost beyond recognition. Many London chambers had, and still have, more or less strong connections with a Circuit, some with more than one. Each set of chambers has a Head, a senior member, usually, but not always, a QC. In the 1960s sets of chambers were much smaller than now. A set with 10 or 12 barristers was large: 20 unheard of.

Each Circuit had a Leader (always a QC), and a junior as his factotum. The office of Circuit Leader was, and remains, a very important and influential one. It may be that the Circuits have varying rules for choosing their Leaders. On the Oxford Circuit the job usually went to the most senior QC with a Circuit practice and was very seldom contested[9]. The Leader is consulted about possible judicial and other appointments on the Circuit, and is *ex officio* a member of the Bar Council. The job lasted on the Oxford Circuit usually until its holder was himself appointed to a full-time job, or retired. The leader of the Midland & Oxford Circuit held office for four years. There was for some years a deputy, who had a strong presumption to the succession, but James Hunt QC abolished the job of deputy when he became leader of the Midland & Oxford, having himself been the deputy.

The Junior, on the other hand, held the job for only a year, during which he or she was the Circuit's convenor and the Leader's right-hand person. Most Circuits nowadays have a separate and semi-permanent Secretary. The Midland Circuit's junior was called the Recorder: on amalgamation with the Oxford

---

9   Last, I am informed by HH Peter Crawford Q.C., in 1953 when there were 3 circuit silks of precisely the same seniority. There was an election, won by George 'Scotty' Baker Q.C. (see page 59 below). I think there may have been another in the late 1980s.

they conceded that the title 'Junior' should be retained for the combined Circuit.

A barrister could be a member of only one Circuit at a time, but could change from one to another. There were strict rules, of the same illogical type as those then obtaining in many trade unions, as to the terms on which a member of a Circuit could appear at a Court on a Circuit other than his own, with curious penalties. These are set out – for those who can be bothered – in Appendix I page 77 seq to this book.

The Circuits performed, and still perform, a valuable regulatory and disciplinary function. You are less likely to be unco-operative to your opponent at Oxford on Monday, if you think you may (as experience shows you certainly *will*) want a favour from the same person at Reading on Wednesday – or from another member of his chambers, who will have been told by your Monday opponent how difficult you were at Oxford.

There were, and of course still are, also sets of chambers in the provinces; mainly in the big cities – Birmingham, Manchester, Liverpool, Leeds etc. Most circuits had rules regulating (usually in effect prohibiting) the opening of sets of chambers, whether free-standing or annexes of London sets, in the smaller towns. The Oxford Circuit had no written rules: its rules were said to reside 'in the breast of the Leader', whence he extracted them when the need arose, consulted them, and then presumably put them back again.

When I came to the Bar in 1960 there were seven Circuits in England and Wales: (alphabetically) the Midland, the North-Eastern, the Northern, the Oxford, the South-Eastern, the Wales and Chester and the Western. It was easy to suppose that that was how it had always been. Not so. Like the states of Central and South-Eastern Europe, the Circuits have quite often changed. The Inner Temple Library possesses a map by one J. Andrews – unfortunately undated, but probably late 18th or early 19th century – showing six English Circuits, including, as well as the

J.Andrews' map of the English and Welsh Circuits
(by courtesy of The Inner Temple)

Midland, the Northern, the Oxford, and the Western, the Norfolk
Circuit (Norfolk, Suffolk, Cambridgeshire, Huntingdonshire
and Bedfordshire) and the Home Circuit (Hertfordshire, Essex,
Kent, Surrey and Sussex), but no North-Eastern; the Northern
then extended *both* sides of the Pennines, and also then included
Cheshire; and four Welsh (North-East, North-West, South-East
and South-West[10]): ten in all. Middlesex, including London, was
not on any Circuit.

---

10   The written evidence of the Welsh Circuit to the Beeching Commission

Until 1939 Wales still had two Circuits, North and South, the former including Cheshire.[11] This no doubt derived from the particular local difficulties of North/South travel in Wales. On the other hand, the old Northern Circuit, (comprising Yorkshire, Lancashire, Durham, Cumberland, Westmoreland and Northumberland) had split itself in two in 1876, because of the volume of work and the size of the population it covered. According to a hallowed story, the Leaders of the two 'new' Circuits tossed a coin to decide which should retain the title Northern: the west won, hence we have now Northern and North-Eastern Circuits, not Northern and North-Western.[12] I do not know when or why Cheshire was moved to the North Wales Circuit.

But for very many years, the south and the west and the centre of England, from Cornwall to Lincolnshire and from Hampshire to Staffordshire, was divided between three Circuits: the Midland, the Oxford and the Western. As Mr. Andrews' map shows, the Midland comprised Beds, Bucks, Northants, Warwickshire, Leicestershire, Derbyshire, Rutland, Nottinghamshire and Lincolnshire; the Oxford comprised Berkshire, Oxfordshire, Gloucestershire, Worcestershire, Herefordshire, Shropshire, Staffordshire and Monmouthshire (then part of England); and the Western comprised Hampshire, Wiltshire, Dorset, Somerset, Devon and Cornwall.

---

names them as the North-West (also known as the Anglesea), the Chester, the Brecon and the Carmarthen. They ought to know!

According to an unauthenticated document in the Circuit papers in the Bodleian Library, it was only in 1831 that English Judges first went the Welsh Circuits. This is corroborated by a statement (also unauthenticated) on pages 140-1 of Vol 2 of Atlay op. cit., to the effect that 'Until ... 1830 all the more important Welsh cases, civil and criminal alike, were tried at Hereford and Shrewsbury'.

11   see Mackinnon op. cit. pp.107 and 197.
12   but see also page 29 infra.

CHAPTER 2

What went wrong

Almost immediately after the end of World War II, for reasons beyond the scope of this book, the criminal statistics began to climb steeply. This is, in a very few words, the main thing that went wrong. The old Court system could not cope with the increase in the number of cases.

As well as more cases, the Courts had to deal with cases lasting longer than before. This was because the extension of criminal legal aid entitled almost every alleged criminal to be legally represented by solicitors and counsel at the public expense. For better or worse, cases tended to last longer. Defending lawyers were able to see legal flaws or weaknesses in a prosecution case that an unrepresented accused person might not see; that was their job. Hence there were more contested cases – and no doubt more acquittals. But it all took longer than it had done in the '30s and '40s.

Liverpool and Manchester.

By the early 1950s there were already serious problems of congestion and delay at the City Quarter Sessions of Liverpool and Manchester. I think this episode should be recorded in some detail, because it can now be seen as an early local solution to what was in truth a national problem, and the very first step towards the end of the Oxford Circuit.

The man who unwittingly lit the fuse which eventually exploded the mine under the old system was a very successful silk on the Northern Circuit, Henry Ince Nelson (always known as 'Harry'). He had a large, mainly civil, practice in the North-West. In accordance with the rules of that Circuit, he had been obliged, on taking silk, to move to London chambers[13] and also

---

13   As it happened, the London chambers he joined on taking silk were the

to move his home to a place more than, I think, 50 miles from any Circuit town. He held in succession a series of well-regarded part-time judicial posts on the Circuit, being Judge of the Salford Hundred Court, and then of the Liverpool Court of Passage (both busy Civil Courts, and both later to be abolished on the Beeching Commission's recommendations). He was probably then destined for the High Court Bench, where a number of his former colleagues were already ensconced.

In 1950 he accepted appointment as the Recorder of Liverpool at the age of 53. Most people, probably including himself, would have regarded that as the last step before he went on the High Court Bench. But it was not to be. He was overwhelmed by the amount of work expected of him as Recorder. Official statistics compiled for the year 1952 showed that the number of persons dealt with at the Liverpool City Quarter Sessions in that year were exactly three times as many as in 1938, the last full year of peace. The Lord Chancellor and the Home Secretary set up a Committee, under the Chairmanship of Sir Alexander Maxwell (a retired civil servant), in December 1952:

> '*to enquire into the need, in order to relieve pressure on Courts of Assize and Quarter Sessions, for the establishment in South Lancashire of a Court on the lines of the Central Criminal Court.*'

With commendable speed it reported in August 1953.[14] Two of its crucial conclusions, in paragraph 61, were that:

> '*There is undue pressure on the City Sessions at Liverpool and Manchester. The volume of work at each of those courts is so large that a Recorder who is in practice at the Bar ought not to be expected to cope with it.*'

and

---

same as those I joined as the junior tenant in 1960. He was seldom seen in chambers, being almost always working in the North-West.

14   Cmnd 8955, 1955/6.

'... in place of the part-time Recorderships at Liverpool and Manchester there should be created two full-time judicial posts ... one being appointed Recorder of Liverpool and the other Recorder of Manchester'.

Harry Nelson had himself given written and oral evidence to the Committee, both representing the Northern Circuit and as Recorder of Liverpool.

Parliament accepted the Maxwell Committee's conclusions and put them into statutory effect reasonably promptly: the Criminal Justice Administration Act 1956 was passed, and came into force, on 28th March 1956. In brief, Part I abolished Liverpool and Manchester City Quarter Sessions (but not their Assizes) and established a new kind of Court with a new name, and a new kind of Judge. It set up a 'Crown Court' in each city with its own *permanent* full-time Judge, still to be called 'the Recorder', as the Committee had proposed, and to sit 'at least eleven times in every year' (Section 1(5)).

Alas, this happened too late for Harry Nelson. In 1954 he had resigned his Recordership after only 4 years, because of the intolerable pressure and weight of the work. (One of his precursors had held the post for 39 years between 1909 and 1948). Nelson was not forgiven: he was not appointed to, though apparently worthy of, the High Court Bench[15]. In 1959 he accepted the relatively obscure and inglorious post of Deputy Commissioner of National Insurance: in 1968 he was promoted to Commissioner. He retired in 1969 and died in 1981.

The Maxwell Commission had been enjoined to consider a 'Central Criminal Court' in South Lancashire: it did so, but rejected the idea. The Central Criminal Court Act 1834, which had established a permanent Court with permanent judges in

---

15   Sir Michael Morland (a Northern Circuiteer and retired High Court Judge) has an alternative explanation, that he (Nelson) was sent to Birmingham to try a long and complex fraud case; but did not come up to expectations in doing so. This does not explain why he chose to resign the Recordership.

the City of London, 122 years earlier (always called the Old Bailey after the street on which it stands) made perhaps the very first departure from the ancient Assize and Quarter Sessions system. The 1834 Act was one of the reforms introduced by Lord Chancellor Brougham, a brilliant man, but so vain that, according to the new *Oxford Dictionary of National Biography*, he faked his death in order to read his own premature obituaries.[16]

The new Crown Courts in Liverpool and Manchester were, on the whole, a success, although they were adversely criticised after only 5 years in the report of another reforming Committee, presided over by Mr. Justice Streatfeild.[17] The qualification is necessary because the two judges appointed were not equally satisfactory. In Manchester Judge Nield QC who, as Mr. Basil Nield QC, M.P. (for Chester) had been a member of the Maxwell Committee, was a definite success. He had been at the Bar in Liverpool. He once reproved my future wife's pupil-master, Basil Gerrard, for having a pupil 'showing too much flesh' in his Manchester Court: she was wearing ¾ length sleeves. In 1960 he was promoted to the High Court Bench, where he was also well-respected. He had the distinction of sitting in every Assize town in England and Wales, and after 1972 he wrote and published a mildly entertaining account of them, with photographs of the Courts and the Judges' Lodgings, called Farewell to the Assizes.

Judge Laski Q.C. who had practised in Manchester, but was appointed to sit in Liverpool, was not such a successful appointment. He was not popular with the local Bar. He also incurred the displeasure of the Court of Criminal Appeal. Convictions in his Court had more than once to be quashed, because he gave the same inappropriate direction to a jury[18],

---

16   Vol 7 page 978.

17   Cmnd 1289/1961.

18   I believe he was in the habit of telling juries that the law relating to the burden and standard of proof was the criminal law's 'signature tune': but I cannot trace any extant report of that. Whatever it was, the Appeal Court did not like it.

despite having been criticised for it in an earlier appeal. He was not promoted to the High Court; he resigned in 1963 and died in 1969.

The late 50's and the 60's

The problems of congestion and delay, which had led to the creation of the Liverpool and Manchester Crown Courts, not surprisingly caused worsening difficulties almost everywhere else, including the Oxford Circuit. The increase of work gave rise to several problems including:

* shortages of proper judges at Borough Quarter Sessions,

* shortages of proper Court rooms and their appurtenances,

* lack of co-ordination between Courts, and inflexibility in the sittings of Assizes.

Quarter Sessions Judges

The pressure of work was such that, when the Recorder of a Borough could not himself sit to deal with it, Deputies and Assistants had to be found to sit in his stead. It has to be said that those who were called on for this purpose were not always of sufficient quality. There were not infrequent misdirections to juries, and mistakes in sentencing. A few Deputies seemed not to have much else to do: in the words of the Book of Common Prayer, justice was sometimes 'indifferently ministered'.[19] This criticism could not be made of two of the Deputies who sometimes sat at Oxford City Sessions, both of whom deserve a mention here.

Max Holdsworth was a short, dapper man, who for some reason always came into Court carrying – not wearing – a pair of white gloves. He used to surprise juries in summing-up by telling them:

---

19   Yes, I know: this is meant to be a slight joke.

'Ladies and gentlemen, the accused doesn't have to give evidence. Indeed it is only in my life-time that an accused person has been able *to give evidence'.*

Max had been born before the Criminal Evidence Act 1898. He had been Recorder of Lichfield for many years, and still had all his marbles.

Fitzwalter Butler was, by contrast, an imposing and bulky figure: for many years, between 1931 and 1973, he edited ten editions of the criminal lawyer's Bible and Vade-mecum, *Archbold*, and so was very knowledgeable. He had an endearing habit of taking a short nap just after the lunch adjournment, and also – less endearing for prosecutors – of intervening in the cross-examination of the accused at the crucial moment with questions which sometimes let him off the hook.

But there were several others who are better forgotten.

Court Rooms

A jury trial needs a surprisingly large number of appropriate rooms. A Court room of sufficient size, a room for the jury, separate robing rooms for the judge and the barristers, and secure accommodation for the accused, to say nothing of the witnesses, the Press and the public, or of appropriate separate sanitary facilities. If the purpose-built Court was not available or was in use for a long case, it was often necessary to use rooms which were certainly not intended for the purpose, in which to deal with other cases.

A striking but enjoyable example of this sometimes happened at Windsor, the Oxford Circuit's closest approach to London. There was no special Court House for the Quarter Sessions of the – pompously entitled – Royal Borough of New Windsor: the Recorder shared a rather shabby Court with the Magistrates. When both were sitting at once, the Quarter Sessions had to find another place; and the place it found was the Windsor Guildhall adjoining the Castle, which has recently had its 15 minutes of fame when the Prince of Wales got re-married there.

It was, and is, an imposing building, obviously not intended to house a Court for jury trials: the walls were lined with stately portraits of long-departed royalty, in massive gilt frames. Proceedings were interrupted twice a day, mid-morning and mid-afternoon, by the military band accompanying the Castle guard playing stirring music as they marched to and from their posts, below the Guildhall's windows. Trials had to come to a halt for a few minutes while the band went past. Sometimes the music gave a witness a welcome opportunity to think of a more plausible answer than he had been about to give as the band approached, while the ancient royals looked down sceptically from their frames on the walls. It was amusing, but it was not really how a Court should be.

In Oxford itself, a second Court was made for the City Sessions out of an attic, up a steep staircase and directly under the roof of the Town Hall. It was another inappropriate and inconvenient Court room, very hot and ill-ventilated in summer; but if the windows were opened, intolerable traffic noise and fumes came up from Blue Boar Street. It was so small that, if you were not careful, the front row of the jury could read your brief: not always desirable.

Similar problems occurred elsewhere; for instance, at Birmingham (where I first sat as a post-Beeching Assistant Recorder) and Stafford, rooms never intended to be used as Courts, were pressed into temporary and unsatisfactory service.

Co-ordination of sittings

I have already mentioned how the use of part-time judges, though in principle unobjectionable and even desirable, in practice resulted in Borough and County Quarter Sessions often sitting at the same time as each other. There was another exacerbating and intractable problem with Assizes.

The authority of the Assize judge to sit at (say) Oxford derived from a royal commission appointing him to sit there, and from the ceremonial reading of the commission[20] aloud by the Clerk of Assize in Court at the opening of the Assize. This ceremony involved much bowing, and the wearing, by the judge, of his full-bottomed wig and the carrying of his tricorn hat, and also the wearing, by the sheriff, of his ceremonial sword, unless the post was held by a woman. Bill Lewis obviously enjoyed reading 'Her Majesty's Commission' in a rich Welsh baritone, at each Assize town from Reading to Newport (Mon.) and Stafford.

The date for this ceremony at each Assize town was fixed by the Lord Chief Justice more than 12 months in advance, before the amount of work to be done there was, or could be, known. Once fixed, the dates could be altered only with much difficulty, because of other uses of the Court,[21] already fixed in advance. So a judge who was due to open the Assizes at Oxford on (say) 1st June, could not start a case of any substance at the previous Assize town (Reading) towards the end of May, in case it did not finish in time for him to get to Oxford by 1st June. Arrears of the longer cases built up: they were often moved from one Assize town to the next, with much inconvenience to local witnesses. Civil cases always had to be taken after the criminal work was finished, and were very frequently 'not reached', with even worse practical problems for litigants, and their lawyers and witnesses.

Some idea of the amazing complexity of the arrangements can be obtained from a perusal of Appendix C to the Streatfeild Committee's report of 1961, where Lord Chief Justice Parker's proposals for reorganization of the Assizes are set out in 8½ pages of detailed analysis and explanation. In the Memorandum from the Lord Chancellor's Office (as it then was) to the Beeching Commission no less than 32 pages and 8 appendices are devoted

---

20   The texts of some of these commissions are printed as appendices to Sir Frank MacKinnon's book, On Circuit, supra., and the procedure is described in detail at pages 47-52.

21   see page 52 below.

to explaining the Assize and Quarter Sessions system in detail. This latter document is available at the British Library, in a volume of selected written evidence submitted to the Commission.

It was a wholly outdated and inefficient system, which gave rise to intolerable delays and inconvenience.

The Oxford and Midland Circuits

Apart from the general problems set out above, there was, in the 1960s, an acrimonious dispute between the Oxford and Midland Circuits about the cases at Birmingham Assizes in which barristers from the Oxford Circuit were entitled to appear, Birmingham being originally in Warwickshire, a Midland Circuit county. The details of this, and other disputes, are set out in Appendix I. At this stage it is necessary only to record that the quarrels were so fierce that they eventually had to be resolved by various Lords Chancellor, who decided them all in the Oxford Circuit's favour. Needless to say, this did not prevent there being at the time a feeling of some coolth between some members of the Circuits, up to and even after the time when the Courts Act 1971 came into force.

Lord Beeching, looking self-satisified
(by courtesy of the National Portrait Gallery)

CHAPTER 3

The Doctor's Remedy

By the mid-sixties the Criminal Courts' problems had got so bad that the Labour government of the day, including Lord Gardiner[22] as Lord Chancellor, resorted to the desperate remedy of appointing a Royal Commission. It was appointed by the Home Secretary, Roy Jenkins, in November 1966:

> *'to inquire into the present arrangements for the administration of justice at Assizes and Quarter Sessions outside Greater London, and to report what reforms should be made ...'*

The chairman of the Commission, Baron (Richard) Beeching D.Phil., was already well-known, even notorious, to the public, having been Chairman of the British Railways Board for a remarkably short period, 1963 to 1965. He had become a national figure of controversy for his drastic and radical surgery of the railway system. He was a doctor of physics by qualification at Imperial College, and an industrial scientist by profession mainly with I.C.I. Having ruthlessly rationalized the railways, for which he was appointed a Life Peer, he returned to I.C.I., as deputy chairman from 1966 to 1968. But from November 1966 to September 1969 he chaired the Royal Commission which, to lawyers of the mid-twentieth century, bears his name. According to Prof. Heuston, Gardiner earned the disapprobation of the prime minister, Harold Wilson, by himself going to Beeching to ask him to take on the job: Wilson thought Gardiner ought to have sent for Beeching.[23]

Beeching's work on the Royal Commission, and its consequences, have earned him precisely one sentence of 25 words in his 3-column entry, plus photograph, in the new *Oxford*

---

22   The erstwhile Head of my pupillage chambers and advocate *sans pareil*.

23   see *Lives of the Lord Chancellors 1940-70* p.227.

Dictionary of National Biography.[24] This reflects the curious fact that Beeching is still firmly connected in the public memory with the pruning of the railways (which were a mere 100 years old, or thereabouts), whereas his part in the total abolition of the 700-year-old Assize and Quarter Sessions system has been almost completely forgotten, even by lawyers.

His fellow commissioners were eight in number; two top businessmen, a senior trades union official, a Queen's Counsel and part-time Judge from the Northern Circuit, a senior London solicitor, a High Court Judge (who had to be replaced by another, on grounds of ill-health: the substitute, Mr. Justice Phillimore, one of the Deputy Chairmen of Oxon Quarter Sessions, was promoted to the Court of Appeal during the Commission's deliberations), a very senior local government official with long experience of Quarter Sessions work in Hampshire, and the Lord Chancellor's Permanent Secretary. They had a very able and proactive secretary, Mr. (later Sir) Derek Oulton: he was to become Permanent Secretary to the Lord Chancellor (1982-1989), having been Deputy Secretary (1972-82). In the latter capacity he signed my letter of appointment as Recorder in 1981. It was a high-powered team.

The National Archives (NA) at Kew possess 440 files of documents, some thick, some thin, relating amongst other matters to the evidence sent to, and the deliberations of, the Commission between 1966 and 1969. These were subject to the 30-year closure rule against public access. In fact they have been available only since 2000[25]. I cannot claim to have read every one of the NA's files: some of the statistical material is not at all reader-friendly. But the four volumes of Minutes of Meetings (LC0 7/236-239) make intermittently riveting reading. Curiously, these seem to be incomplete: the last extant Minute (of the 40th meeting in May

---

24 Vol. 4 pp.809-10.

25 It is not clear why Files LC07/431 and 438, which consist *solely* of contemporary press-cuttings, were ever 'closed' at all!

'69) appears to contemplate at least one other meeting; but none is recorded, even though publication was still 4 months away.

At the first meeting, on 25th November 1966, Lord Beeching expressed the hope that they would report within 12 months: in fact it took them nearly 3 times as long. Eighteen months later, on the 24th meeting in April 1968, Lord Beeching is recorded as saying that his

'experience with British Rail had shown that sensible proposals, which had been generally accepted when they were first made, were gradually eroded by irrational and strongly-backed local opposition to points of detail'.

He seems to have learned not to allow that to happen again.

The general effect of the evidence – from judges, barristers, solicitors and numerous organizations of all shapes and sizes – was that Yes, the system had serious problems: but No, it did not necessarily need to be wholly abolished; it could still be made to work. Mr. Oulton, and his assistant Mrs. Vera Demmery, prepared a remarkable analysis of the evidence (LC07/299) which showed overwhelming support for the view that both Assizes and Quarter Sessions were defective, but more evenly divided opinion on the question whether the defects were remediable. A narrow majority thought Assizes *could* be put right: a similarly narrow majority thought Quarter Sessions could not. It was a Gordian knot, and Lord Beeching had learned from Alexander the Great how to deal with it.

Most of the Commission worked hard. They met almost every month, sometimes twice, and, in both July '67 and '68, three times in a month: sometimes to receive oral evidence, more often to deliberate.

A note in the correspondence file, LC07/230 of April 1969 raised the curious question whether one of the two business-men on the Commission (no pack-drill here) should not be invited to sign the Report, because of the small contribution he had made;

I think his company was involved in a take-over battle. But Civil Service discretion thought better of that. All nine names appear at the foot of the Report. There were no dissenters.

As one would expect, the Report went through several drafts, at least six. One was substantially drafted by the Commission's Secretary and Mrs. Demmery, at the members' request.[26] But, strangely, only one of these drafts seems to have survived, an early draft dated August 1967.[27] This is only 39 pages long and contains many blank spaces. It includes no reference to either the Oxford Circuit or its abolition. Indeed, there are scarcely any references in either the working papers, or the published Report, to the Oxford Circuit, other than as part of a factual account of the existing state of affairs. The following has therefore to be reproduced in full, from a document in the correspondence file LC07/230:

> *'The Oxford Circuit (my own), which will dislike your proposals very much, may seize on the last sentence of this paragraph as meaningless. What does 'serve' mean? Incidentally the case you make for the abolition of that circuit is very powerful and I am sure you are right not to descend into detailed argument'.*

This cryptic note, with which the recipient has indicated agreement by a large pencil tick in the margin, is part of a long document dated 17th April 1969 signed 'J.M.C.S.', whom I have provisionally identified as John Michael Cartwright Sharp, secretary to the Law Commission 1968-78, (and the son of a Leader of the Oxford Circuit in the 1940s). The Law Commission is a statutory body charged with Law Reform; it was the brain-child of Lord Chancellor Gardiner. He (J.M.C.S.) was, I think, writing to Lord Beeching, and was commenting in that note on para. 171 of *another* draft of the Report. This draft, tantalisingly, has not survived. Para 171 of the published Report has nothing at

---

26   see Minutes of Meeting of January 1968: para 325.

27   LC07/440.

all to do with the Oxford Circuit; and the 'case' for its abolition is not made anywhere, powerfully or otherwise; nor does the Report 'descend into detailed argument' about it. The Circuit's abolition is simply assumed as a *fait accompli*. Cartwright Sharp's advice was taken with a vengeance.

A puzzling note elsewhere in the working papers at NA states that the 'North-Western Circuit' is to be called 'the Northern', and the new, amalgamated Circuit 'the Oxford and Midland'.

As a long-serving President of Mental Health Review Tribunals (1995 to date) I am all too familiar with the symptoms of paranoid delusions. The reader will have to make his or her own diagnosis. But what is one to make of the following?

(a) An early draft of the Report (LC0 7/440) does not propose the abolition of or any alteration to the Oxford, or any other, Circuit;

(b) a late draft (before April 69) which is not now with the NA papers must have 'made the case for the abolition of the (Oxford) Circuit' very powerfully: see J.M.C.S.'s comments on it in LC0 7/230 above; but this 'very powerful case' has been deleted from the Report published six months later;

(c) several other drafts of the Report are also absent from the NA files;

(d) the Minutes of Meetings 1-40 contain no reference to any discussion about the abolition of the Oxford Circuit, though they do include copious records of discussions about *other* Circuits, in particular the Wales & Chester. Until a very late stage, the Commission were minded to propose that the Wales & Chester also be abolished and divided between the Western and the Northern Circuits, because the size of its population did not meet the Commission's criterion for a 'regional centre'. Strong and predictable indignation west of Offa's Dyke eventually prevailed over this idea: and in the end the Welsh Circuit even gained

Monmouthshire ... from the Oxford. But the Report in this instance did 'descend into detailed argument' about it: see paras 295-297, where the decision to retain the Circuit is said to have been reached 'not without reluctance'.

(e)   the published report contains (para 288 seq.) detailed accounts of the ancient Courts in Bristol, Norwich, Salford and Liverpool, and the Commission's approach to them and their proposed abolition, and of the problems the Commission had with the South-Eastern, the Western, and the Wales and Chester Circuits, but absolutely no reference to the Oxford or its abolition.

What was it about our Circuit and the proposal to abolish it, that caused the Commission to change its mind (? twice) about whether to mention it or not? What had we done – apart from entertaining his Lordship at a Circuit Dinner at Oxford - to deserve unexplained oblivion? Why should the Commission apparently wish to avoid explicit reference to one of its main recommendations concerning the organisation of the Courts in the provinces, and the consequences for the Bar? Even the Bar Council was part of the conspiracy (says the paranoid patient) to down-grade the Oxford Circuit. The statistics it supplied to Beeching wrongly allotted *all of* the Birmingham Bar to the Midland, and thus reduced the Oxford's manpower by about 40, or 30%, and increased the Midland's correspondingly. Obviously my medication should be increased.

The Commission reported to the Lord Chancellor and Parliament in September 1969. The report, together with its appendices and index, occupies 183 pages in Volume 28 of the Parliamentary Papers for 1968-9, sandwiched between the annual report of the Board of Trade, relating to the control of office development, and the Report and Accounts of the Criminal Injuries Compensation Board for the year to 31st March 1968. It is not easy to find, even in a law library. But, once found, it is a readable and impressive document.

Chapter I (like my Chapter 1 above) describes the system as it then was, supplemented by the Appendices at the end of the Report. Appendix 1 lists the witnesses and organisations from whom it had received written or oral evidence. Remarkably, the Midland Circuit was the only Circuit to submit no evidence (see page 148). Appendix 3, which sets out the towns where Assizes and Quarter Sessions sat, listed by Circuits, does not show that the Oxford Circuit had had, for 80 and more years, the right to appear at Birmingham Assizes from their inception in 1883. This is a surprising, and I fear a damaging, error (page 158). Appendix 5 confirms the remarkable rise in the case-load of work, comparing 1938 with each year from 1957 to 1967: an approximate 3-fold increase from 10,003 to 30,265 in the number of persons tried at Assizes, the Old Bailey, the two existing Crown Courts, and Quarter Sessions: and Appendix 6 shows a more than 10-fold increase in the numbers of persons granted legal aid. Perhaps most remarkably, Appendix 12 shows the fall and rise in the numbers of the practising Bar between 1953 and 1968: falling from 2010 in 1954 to 1919 in 1960, and thereafter rising every year to 2,379 in 1968. (In 2004 the corresponding number was 11,564, an increase of more than 200 over 2003, and of more than six-fold during my 40+ year professional lifetime.)

Chapter II of the Report contains a trenchant account of 'The Merits and Defects of the Present Pattern of Courts' – mostly its defects. These included the absence of co-ordination between, and the inflexibility in, the sittings of the various Courts, the inadequacy of many court buildings and their facilities, and the lack of correspondence between the demand for the Courts' time and attention, and the supply of those services, where and when they were in demand.

Inconspicuously, in Chapter III, para. 167 on page 62 the first clear indication of the Oxford Circuit's doom can be seen. Having rightly stated in para. 14 that there are *seven* circuits, and listed them and their Courts in Appendix 3, the report points out that there are *six* major conurbations, measured by population, in England and Wales, centring on London, South Lancashire, Birmingham, Leeds, Bristol and Cardiff[28]. None of these, nor even any of the next five in descending order, was wholly an Oxford Circuit town or city.

Chapter IV sets out, in four brief but crucial pages, the Outline of the new system the Commission is to recommend. Paragraph 176(b)-(e) proposes a 'new permanent bench of Circuit judges' consisting of 'all existing County Court judges' plus 'sufficient additional whole-time appointments', supplemented by 'some part-time judges, to be called Recorders'. Then in subparagraph (f), at the foot of page 65 of the Report, comes the Oxford Circuit's death sentence, contained (one might almost say, concealed) in the apparently innocuous proposal that two High Court judges, to be called Presiding Judges, shall have 'special responsibility for each of six circuits'. This, I believe, is the first point in the Report at which the proposed reduction of the number of circuits is made explicit. A less than well-informed reader could be forgiven for thinking that that sub-paragraph meant what it said, and only what it said. One page later, at the foot of page 66, in paragraph 180, appears this passage:-

'For administrative purposes, and particularly to co-ordinate the use of judge power and other resources we propose that all Court centres shall be grouped into six areas which we refer to as Circuits. Each Circuit will include at least one main centre of population ...'

Thus the Oxford Circuit was to be sacrificed on the altar of administrative convenience.

Chapters V, VI and VII contain the Commission's more detailed proposals for reforming the Courts and the judiciary respectively. Assizes and Quarter Sessions (both County and Borough) are to be abolished. New Crown Courts, on the model

---

28   Cardiff only just got in, to make the sixth. At fairly early stages (eg Meetings 21 & 30) in its deliberations the Commission counted *five* conurbations on which to base the 'Regions'.

of, and with the same name as, those in Liverpool and Manchester, are to replace them. There are to be permanent 'Circuit' Judges (a new title, paradoxical and confusing, because they were not to go 'on circuit') sitting in them, with the still-itinerant High Court Judges in the big cities. The travelling Clerks of Assize are also to be abolished, along with their staff, and the hampers.

This was exactly the opposite conclusion to that reached by the Streatfeild Committee, only 8 years earlier. The Commission's Secretaries in February 1967[29] had found overwhelming support in South Lancashire for their 'new' Crown Courts.[30] (The Commission had had great difficulty in deciding on the name of the new Court. At one time, the title 'The Criminal Court' found favour, but was later dropped.) Some Crown Courts are to be more equal than others: three tiers of higher or lower status are proposed. Many towns are to lose their ancient courts, or to have their courts reduced in status.[31]

The abolition of the Oxford Circuit is nowhere explicitly spelt out even here, but it is again implicit in paragraph 286 which lists 6 circuits, a list from which the name 'Oxford' is absent, and in the map of the proposed Circuits on the facing page where the Oxford Circuit simply does not appear. Paragraph 287 refers to 'some disturbance of the Bar' and 'a violation of sentiment', but goes on to express the view that 'the difficulties will be short-lived and the longer term effect will be wholly beneficial'. This seems, to a not unbiased reader, like an impenitent rapist's inexpert attempt at a plea in mitigation. The paragraph goes on to refer to 'the new Circuits': but there are to be no new Circuits, only one fewer of the old ones.

A new kind of Recorder is proposed. The existing attachment of an individual to a Borough is to be abolished 'with regret'.

---

29 Judge Laski Q.C. had retired 4 years earlier!

30 see LC07/257.

31 pages 96 & 97.

The new Recorder is to be an all-purpose part-timer, attached to a circuit, but only administratively (para 239 seq.).

It is tempting, if not compelling, to think, especially in the light of Cartwright Sharp's note, that the failure of the report to announce in clear terms the abolition of the Oxford Circuit was deliberate: but why?[32] They cannot have thought that it would pass unnoticed. It is inconsistent with what one can infer of Beeching's own confrontational character, that he might have thought he would 'lose the argument', if he raised it. Alone of the pre-1972 Circuits, the Oxford Circuit does not even appear in the Report's Index: an unpleasantly sinister, Orwellian omission.

Even so, it would be unrealistic and sentimental to argue that Beeching was wrong. The old regime had to go: it could not be tinkered with any more. The new system had to be based on the great centres of population, not on the old county and borough boundaries. The Oxford Circuit, described in 1951 by Bosanquet[33] as 'a country circuit', did not include any such great centre. The cathedral cities of Oxford, Gloucester, Worcester and Hereford, though providing admirable settings for judicial panoply and ceremony, and recently in the case of Oxford, for television murders and detectives, could not produce the weight of criminal litigation to justify the Circuit's continuance ... but it would have been more satisfactory, and much less ungracious, if they had said so!

---

32   Sir Derek Oulton Q.C. (the Commission's Secretary, now retired) has been courteously unable to provide any answer to this question, despite my importunate enquiry.

33   op. cit. p.11.

CHAPTER 4

Taking the Medicine:
The first gulp; the Bill & the Act.

The report was published late in September 1969. It cost 17 shillings and 6 pence (that is 87 1/2 new pence). A bargain; less than the price of a litre of unleaded petrol at the time of writing. Lord Beeching held a press conference; and, judging from the press coverage which followed, he did well. I have not found *any* adverse comment in any press report – whether tabloid, broadsheet or legal. The death sentence on the Oxford Circuit went entirely, but understandably, unremarked. The proposed abolition of a system which had served the country well for some 7 centuries, but had at last broken down irretrievably, was greeted with universal acclamation and approval, and without a word of regret. The House of Commons joined in the chorus of welcome in a debate in May 1970.

In the very next month, the Labour Government, which had appointed the Commission, was defeated in a General Election. The Lord Chancellor in Edward Heath's new Government was Lord Hailsham, and the Attorney-General Sir Peter Rawlinson QC. Both of them espoused the Beeching proposals, almost unchanged. The Courts Bill was introduced by Lord Hailsham in the House of Lords at about 3.30 pm on the 10th of November 1970. Considering that the Report was only 14 months old, this was good going by the draftsmen of a very radical piece of legislation, dealing with statutes passed as long ago as the reign of Henry VIII (see Schedule 11, Parts II and IV), and various others only slightly less ancient.

The Bill was debated in the House of Lords on a number of occasions in November and December 1970. It was unanimously welcomed by Lords Gardiner, Parker C.J., Dilhorne (a former Lord Chancellor), Denning M.R. and others. The only note of controversy was struck, quite hard and often, by some solicitor peers (Fletcher and Goodman in particular) on the question of solicitors' supposed 'rights' of audience in the new Court, and to appointment as circuit judges.

The Bill's passage through the House of Commons was equally uneventful. Such controversy as there was related to the same vexed questions of the 'rights' of solicitors to appointment to the Circuit Bench, and to appear in the Crown Court. This was a topic the Beeching Commission had (pardonably) fought shy of, doubting whether it was within its terms of reference. In the event solicitors can be said to have gained some ground in the legislation – see Section 12; but they did not make much use of their enhanced position. Bearing in mind the *present* Lord Chancellor's extraordinary policy of regular reductions in the remuneration of lawyers in the Crown Court from the public purse, this is not *now* surprising. At the time, the issue was regarded by many as involving the probable end of civilization as we then knew it. It was also, less cataclysmically, predicted that any extension of solicitors' rights would mean that 'nobody would come to the Bar in the future'. Both proved false; the world went on, and numbers at the Bar went on climbing steeply. So much for prediction. At no stage in either House was the demise of the Oxford Circuit mentioned.

The Courts Bill received the Royal Assent on the 12th May 1971. Her Majesty, or her appropriate deputy, did a lot of assenting that day. Some 10 other Bills became Acts, ranging from Animals to the Coinage. The Courts Act did not come into force on the date it was passed. As Lord Hailsham had hoped when introducing the Bill in December 1970, it came into force on the 1st January 1972[34]. The Act has 59 Sections and 11 Schedules, which contain nearly 150 paragraphs. It occupies 111 pages in the Queen's Printers' copy of the Statutes: 20 of those pages are Schedule 11, the repeals.

---

34   As is the way with modern statutes, it did not last long. Much of it was repealed, and re-enacted, by the Supreme Court Act 1981, with effect from 1st January 1982.

Lord Beeching's job was now done. He had returned briefly to I.C.I., but left in disappointment at not becoming Chairman. However he soon found somewhere else to sit: the Chair of Redland Ltd, which he occupied until 1984. He died in the following year.

A curious fact about the Courts Act is that new legislation was not required to effect many of the changes to the Assizes which occurred on 1st January 1972. Sections 70 to 77 of the Supreme Court of Judicature (Consolidation) Act 1925 had given the Sovereign wide powers to direct by Order in Council where and when Courts of Assize should sit and ...

> *'for the discontinuance, either temporarily or permanently and either wholly or partially of any former circuit and the formation of any new circuit by the union of any counties or parts of counties ... '.*[35]

It may be that the Parliamentary Draftsman thought these provisions did not extend to the *total* abolition of Assizes, based as they always had been upon counties. New legislation was obviously needed in any event, both for the abolition of Quarter Sessions, and to create the new Crown Court, its judiciary and administration.

So it was that on the 1st January 1972 'at the midnight hour while the world slept' (to quote Pandit Nehru) the venerable institutions of Assizes[36] and Quarter Sessions, and with them, the Oxford Circuit, passed into history.

The Second gulp; the Judges.

There was much to do in the intervening 7½ months between mid-May 1971 and January 1972. In particular a sufficiency

---

35   see Section 72(1)(a).

36   Ironically, the very last Assize in England & Wales was held in December 1971 on the Oxford Circuit at Gloucester.

of Circuit Judges and Recorders had to be appointed. The Act provided (in Schedule 2 Part I) that a number of existing Judges should 'on the appointed day' (i.e. 1st January 1972) become Circuit Judges. These included in particular the Judges of the Old Bailey, the Recorders of Liverpool and Manchester, all the existing County Court Judges (about 90), and about a dozen other full-timers.

The Commission had calculated that about 40 new appointments of Circuit Judges would be needed (para. 236). The Lord Chancellor's Department went about this process with, I believe, some subtlety, even cynicism. In the '50s and '60s it had been uncommon for a county court judge to be promoted to the High Court, even one who sat (as many did) to do criminal work at the County Quarter Sessions,. Appointment as a county court judge was regarded as an end in itself, and quite a pleasant and often undemanding end as well. In the pre-1972 days, the longest-serving county court judge for the time being was knighted, honoris causa, (and the senior judge of the Queen's Bench Division was appointed a Privy Councillor).

The creation of the new rank of Circuit Judge, with a status and a salary (£8,300) and pension higher than that of a County Court Judge, but not as high as those of the High Court, brought about a new, probably unprecedented, situation where so many appointments were needed at once. A Circuit judge was not to get a knighthood and would not be entitled (except at the Old Bailey) to be addressed as 'my Lord'. His robes were to be, and they remain, purple, not red[37]. The Department must have been understandably uncertain whether the job, and its rewards and perquisites would attract 40 barristers of the right calibre, and the right age or seniority.

In order to tempt the waverers, in particular those who had further ambitions, which included a knighthood and a red, rather

---

37 Red robes were bestowed on Senior Circuit Judges, a rank created at a later stage, upon Circuit Judges with special responsibilities in the big cities.

than merely purple, 'dressing gown', Lord Chancellor Hailsham in April 1971 promoted two County Court Judges to the High Court Bench – both of whom, I hasten to say, were conspicuously successful in their elevated positions. It is my belief that this was done, when it was done, in order to indicate to the ambitious waverers that acceptance of a Circuit judgeship might well lead on to fortune, to a K (or a D!) and to the red robes of the High Court. Only two had been promoted in the previous six years.

One[38] of those who took the bait was Kenneth Mynett QC, a Birmingham practitioner and a former solicitor, who took silk in 1960, and was the Recorder of Stoke-on-Trent. He led for the prosecution in the Reading Juke-Box Case (see Appendix II). On the coming into force of the Courts Act on 1st January 1972, he accepted a Circuit judgeship and became the first full-time judge of the Oxford Crown Court, sitting in the Town Hall Court of the former City Quarter Sessions. I believe I appeared before him there in his very first case in that capacity. He was then wearing his black, silk's robes (but with a judge's wig). He was still wearing them (or replacements) twelve years later, when he died in office. It was unkindly said that he expected his service on the Circuit Bench to be so brief, before promotion to the High Court, that he thought he would have been wasting his money buying purple robes.

There was regrettable tension between him and the former Recorder of Oxford, Brian Gibbens QC, then one of the Joint Leaders of the Midland & Oxford Circuit, and a much-loved and -respected figure. The problem arose out of the use of the two Courts in the Town Hall (see page 21 above). When Brian was sitting (as a new-style Recorder) at Oxford and Kenneth was also sitting as the new Circuit Judge, both men felt it *infra dig* to sit in the poky upstairs Court (see pages 14 & 15). I forget how the

---

38   Others who did so from the Oxford Circuit included Michael Talbot (pp.5 supra & 42 infra) and James Irvine (p.52 infra): both, I'm sure, with no further ambitions.

Brian Gibbens QC, trying not to laugh
(by courtesy of Oxford Crown Court)

immediate problem was resolved. In due course it was arranged
that they sat in Oxford on different days.

Kenneth was a good, if quite severe, judge. He had the knack
of imposing sentences (many on clients of mine) right at the top
of the unappealable range. Socially, he was rather less agreeable.
He enrolled as a mature student in a course in European Law at
the University, but according to one of my former tutors, he was
not a successful pupil. When one went into his private room at
Court (for example, to deal with a bail application in Chambers),
he would greet one with a smile and a sigh, and would regretfully
lay aside a heavy tome on Brussels jurisprudence, and pick up
the grubby manila file containing the bail papers.

The same topic produced some covert hilarity when, towards the end of a 2-week trial of an affray[39], the Bar (about 15 of us) entertained him to dinner in Oxford. John Baker Q.C., who was prosecuting, mischievously organised a sweepstake on the length of time that would elapse between his arrival and his first reference to Europe. We all duly made our bets. Kenneth fooled us all. Literally as he took off his overcoat, he said to John and me 'I'm sorry I'm a little late. I was detained by an urgent telephone call from Gordon about the conference next month in Luxembourg'. He was of course referring to Gordon (now Lord) Slynn, at that time the UK Advocate-General at the European Court. All the bets were off, amid much mirth; nobody had selected zero.

His portrait now hangs in Court 1 in the new Crown Court in St. Aldates: he is of course wearing a silk's, not a judge's, full-dress attire – black robes, lace cuffs and jabot and full-bottomed wig. When the first verdict of Not Guilty was returned there, the picture is said to have fallen off the wall.

Portrait of HH Judge Mynett QC, in Court 1 in St Aldates' (photograph by the author)

---

39   This was a quite entertaining case, where the Slough Hell's Angels came to Oxford to have a fight with the Oxford Chapel. Their intelligence was poor; the Oxford Chapel had been disbanded. So the Slough group started their own fight at the Pear Tree Roundabout Cafe, north of Oxford, only to be confronted – and routed – by a well-disciplined Rugby team returning from an away game in the West Country.

Brian Gibbens was shabbily treated by the Lord Chancellor's Department. On the coming into force of the Courts Act 1971, all existing Recorderships (his being Oxford, as we have seen) and all appointments as Chairman and deputies of County Sessions (his also being Oxon) were to lapse. But barrister holders of such offices were automatically appointed new-style Recorders, *so long as they applied*. Brian and several others, including the admirable Michael Maguire Q.C., leader of the Northern Circuit, declined to apply. They took the view that, as Parliament had abolished their jobs for which I think they had *not* applied, but had been appointed, if the Department wanted their services, it was for the Department to ask for them. During the autumn of 1971 long lists of appointments (including a few solicitors) appeared in the Press, but Brian's name was never among them, until very late in the year he was, one felt rather grudgingly, appointed a Recorder.

Brian was again badly, even farcically, treated shortly thereafter. Having been appointed Joint Leader of the new Midland & Oxford Circuit with the Midland's leader, Michael Davies QC, he was conspicuously passed over when Michael Davies was appointed to the High Court Bench in early 1973 (a very good appointment), but Brian wasn't. He became sole leader of the recently combined Circuit. Then the Press carried the news of the appointment to the Circuit Bench of T.B. Gibbens. Brian was showered with letters of congratulations. He had to send them back. It wasn't him. Terry Gibbens was an obscure London criminal hack and a poor judge. I think Evelyn Waugh's 'Scoop' came true, and the wrong person (with the right name) was appointed by mistake.

It did not end there. He was eventually, in late 1973, appointed to the Circuit Bench, but had to spend a purgatorial period sitting in the judicial slums at the Inner London Crown Court. At last he was found a post nearly worthy of his abilities and status, when appointed one of the permanent judges of the Old Bailey, where he found two old friends and former colleagues, Alan King-

Hamilton and Charles Lawson (see Appendix II below) already well-established. His former colleagues and friends from the Oxford Circuit felt that, having had his Circuit abolished under him, without explanation, he deserved better.

I venture to reproduce here the supplemental obituary note following his death in November 1985, which I wrote and The Times obligingly published, but disobligingly cut. The part the sub-editor amputated is in square brackets at the end of what follows:

"Your obituary notice on His Honour Brian Gibbens QC (Nov. 9), in dwelling on his judicial years at the Old Bailey, made only the briefest reference to his other professional distinction – his association with Oxford Circuit.

"For a now middle-aged generation of circuiteers, Brian was the embodiment, and the life and soul, of the Circuit. He practised throughout its length and breadth – from Reading to Newport, from Stafford to Gloucester – in every sort of case.

"He was successively Recorder of West Bromwich, and of Oxford and was the Leader of the Circuit from 1966 until amalgamation with the Midland in 1972, whereupon he became joint (and later sole) Leader of the new Midland and Oxford Circuit.

"He was a marvellous raconteur with an unrivalled repertoire of hilarious circuit anecdotes. His jovial presence would invariably enliven the dreariest robing room [or the most tedious train journey: he presided as Leader over many convivial circuit occasions, and – with sorrow – over its lamented demise as a separate entity. He was much missed on circuit when he took up his arduous duties in London]."

The Third Gulp: the Circuits.

The Oxford Circuit took its proposed abolition, and merger with the Midland, on the chin. There was an Extraordinary Meeting on Saturday 6th December 1969 at Lincoln's Inn at 11.15 (with lunch at 1 p.m: price 15 shillings (75 pence)), to consider what could be salvaged, including the name 'Oxford', the position of those circuiteers whose practices would straddle the new boundaries and of the local Bar at Newport (Mon.), and various other transitional problems.

We had a commemorative photograph taken in front of the Law Courts and a (semi-) final[40] dinner in the Inns of Court, at which Brian Gibbens and Alan King-Hamilton made moving and indignant speeches. The two circuits met each other in joint plenary session in the Inner Temple Hall on a Saturday morning late in 1971. We got on well, despite the earlier disagreements. Messrs. Gibbens and Davies were appointed joint leaders by acclamation. After Michael Davies' appointment to the High Court Bench, Brian became sole leader, and was himself succeeded by a series of very satisfactory leaders, of whom Douglas Draycott Q.C. was the first former Oxford circuiteer.

Douglas was a delightfully laid-back character. He had a comfortably furnished narrow boat, in which he sometimes lived, when appearing at a Court near a convenient canal. He also took her on holiday to Paris, and moored close to the Hotel de Ville on the Canal St. Martin. I am pleased to say his son Simon, a former member of my chambers, is a very successful Circuit silk. Another Oxonian Leader was Peter Weitzman Q.C., a charming, compelling and elegant advocate, with the most beautiful handwriting I ever saw.

It was not simply a matter of amalgamating the two Circuits 'as they were'. *Both* lost territory, by administrative decree. The Oxford Circuit lost Berkshire and part of Oxfordshire to the South-

---

40   '(Semi-)final' because we had another dinner -- convened by John Murchie (see Appendix II below) 25 years later – for the survivors.

Eastern, Gloucestershire to the Western, and Monmouthshire to the Welsh; and the Midland lost Buckinghamshire to the South-Eastern[41]. Worse was to follow. The Oxford Circuit had, following the December '69 meeting, made written representations to the Lord Chancellor in January 1970 asking (a) that Oxford and Reading should be on the same circuit, and (b) that Oxford should retain Tier 1 status (that is, to deal with both the most serious criminal and civil work, with a visiting High Court Judge). The first of these requests was refused, but as later events proved, only for the time being; Reading went, with Berkshire, to the South-Eastern. But the second was, for the moment, granted. As time has passed, the pressure to down-grade Oxford has increased. If only there had been in fact the number of interesting murders that Detective Chief Inspector Morse had to deal with in fiction, it might have been different. But Oxford is still (just) a Tier 1 Court.

To the fastidious Civil Service mentality, the fact that the remnant of Oxfordshire stuck out topographically southwards from the rest of the Midland & Oxford Circuit, if not like a sore thumb, then like Florida from the rest of the U.S.A., could not be allowed to continue. The *coup de grace* came in March 2001 when, by a stroke[42] of the administrative pen, Oxford itself and the rest of Oxfordshire was moved to the South-Eastern Circuit, and, reasonably enough, shortly thereafter the Circuit decided to drop the words '& Oxford' from its title.

R.I.P.

---

41 According to Sir Michael Davies, Lord Gardiner, another former Midland circuiteer, suggested that the 'new' joint Circuit be called simply The Midland. But he was by then no longer Lord Chancellor, and we agreed to be called the Midland and Oxford. It was only a temporary stay of execution.

42 This stroke was resisted, but to no avail, by various senior members of the M & O Circuit, including its leaders at the time, James Hunt Q.C., a graduate of Keble College, Oxford, and, from October 1999, Rex Tedd Q.C. Lord Chancellor Irvine had been at Cambridge. A recent attempt by the Civil Servants to do even worse violence to the Western Circuit, by removing Winchester and Hampshire to the voracious South Eastern Circuit, has, at least for the time being, been defeated by very high-powered opposition.

CHAPTER 5

What we have lost

What we have lost can, perhaps rather snobbishly, be encapsulated in the contrast between the different venues for the annual summer parties of the Oxford Circuit and the transitional Midland and Oxford Circuit on the one hand, and the 'new' Midland Circuit on the other. The Oxford Circuit always had a Grand Night Dinner, sometimes expanded into a Ball, at one of the Oxford colleges. I recall delightful evenings at Lincoln College – this is a rare compliment from a graduate of its rival and neighbour college, Brasenose – at Univ. where we entertained, and I wholly failed to recognise, the venerable Professor Goodhart[43], and at Christ Church[43], where we entertained the all-too-recognizable Lord Beeching. Compare those occasions with the venue for the Midland Circuit's Ball in 2005, the International Convention Centre, Birmingham, and you will begin to see what we have lost.

Pursuant to para 283 of the Beeching report, we have lost the Courts where Abingdon, Banbury, Newbury and Windsor Quarter Sessions were held, each of which deserves a few words of recollection. I have referred to Windsor Sessions' claim on posterity above.

Abingdon was bound to lose its Court. After all, it had not even got a railway station: but then, who was it who in another capacity had closed the delightful little branch line from Appleford Halt to Abingdon? The Court had been held in a fine, probably medieval, building, which had no sort of ante-chamber or entrance hall, only a curtained alcove just inside the street door. So a belated witness would, not infrequently, throw open the door and blunder through the curtain, loudly cursing the weather or the traffic, only to find himself at once confronted by the Recorder, a jury and assorted lawyers in mid-trial.

---

43   It may have been Pembroke College.

Abingdon also lacked a barristers' robing room: we put on our wing collars, bands, wigs and gowns in the Mayor's parlour, where the Borough's historic plate glowed in glass-fronted cupboards.

Abingdon was lucky in its Recorders. The last of the line was Patrick Medd QC, the most charming and versatile of silks, whose memorial service filled Dorchester Abbey. He was preceded by the famous dandy, Stephen Benson, appointed in 1929, of whom was told the celebrated anecdote about the jury which included the Wykeham Professor of Logic from Oxford. The story goes that after a careful summing-up from Benson, explaining the doctrine of recent possession in a larceny case (whereby guilt might be inferred from possession of the swag shortly after its removal), the Professor sent a written question to the Recorder asking him to expand upon the distinction between a deduction and an inference. Benson passed the buck to Robert Hutton who was prosecuting (see page 8 above) and invited his comments. Hutton at once replied 'I have always understood, Sir, that a deduction is what one deduces, whereas an inference is what one infers'. 'Quite right, Mr. Hutton' said the Recorder, 'I entirely accept what you say. (To the jury) That's clear enough for you isn't it, ladies and gentlemen?' The rest of the jury must have got the message; there was no appeal from the conviction that followed.[44]

Banbury Quarter Sessions was held in a spacious upper chamber of the Town Hall, an elderly building in the town centre, and the jury sat in a free-standing wooden structure, which was curved, so that the back row of benches was longer than the front. On one famous occasion an unusually numerate lawyer noticed, half way through a trial, that there were seven jurors in the back row and six in the front: consternation. Neither the Recorder, Michael Talbot,[45] nor the barristers in the case could find any

---

44 An alternative school of thought has the roles of Benson and Hutton reversed and the Court Reading or Gloucester, not Abingdon. Both men had a dry forensic wit: the truth will never now be known.

45 see pages 5 above and 42 below.

lawful solution in Archbold or elsewhere. So the too-numerous jury was discharged and they had to start again.

Newbury Quarter Sessions had been presided over since 1935 by its Recorder, Edward Terrell Q.C., a most remarkable character. He was notorious for prolonging cases far beyond any advance estimate, in order, it was unkindly suggested, to give himself enough to do. He also sought to enhance his status by adopting the forms and ceremonies of the Assizes: he had his warrant of appointment read aloud by the Clerk of the Peace at the beginning of every session, he had his nephew sit with him on the bench and described him as his 'marshall', and he referred to his room at the local Trust House Hotel as his 'lodgings'. After 1971 he became the *Honorary* Recorder of Newbury, pursuant to Section 54 of the Courts Act 1971, a peculiar and Gilbertian distinction in the absence of a Court, of which he was obviously anxious that posterity should not be unaware. The entry he composed in *Who Was Who* mentions it twice.[46]

This entry leads to something else that we have lost, namely Circuit Indictments. On the Circuit's abolition, our last junior, Paul Clark – later to be a Circuit Judge in Oxford and Lent Reader of the Middle Temple in 2005 – was directed by our last leader, Brian Gibbens, to deposit its archives at the Bodleian Library, where they occupy several dozen files. The file of Minutes of Circuit Meetings is wonderfully uninformative. By far the thickest file contains the Circuit Indictments. These record the occasions upon which a member of the Circuit in some way or other came to public, rather than merely professional, attention, whether favourable or unfavourable. The Indictments were prosecuted after dinner at Grand Nights, often in Oxford, when first the accused would be prosecuted and then his case would, by another speaker, be aggravated. Both speeches were addressed to the Circuit Junior. There was a very particular rhetorical skill in this. Several circuiteers were expert at it. Brian Gibbens himself

---

46   Vol VII page 783.

and Richard Tucker were very good, but best of all was Michael Underhill – his comic timing was unsurpassed. There was also much skill in the drafting of these Indictments, as there is in drafting real ones. *Archbold* was scoured for obscure and possibly relevant, but always amusing, offences: the Circuit Junior had the job of drafting the Indictments. Nobody was ever known to have been acquitted. The penalty was always expressed in dozens of port for the Circuit Cellars.

Edward Terrell was prosecuted by the circuit in 1958. During WWII he had distinguished himself by inventing at least two interesting and valuable devices, which of course are specified in his entry in *Who Was Who*. These were 'Plastic armour fitted to 10,000 Allied War and Merchant ships 1940-44' and the 'first Allied rocket bomb for attacks on U-Boat Shelters' for the first of which, according to *Who Was Who*, he received an award from the Royal Commission on Awards to Inventors (1949). Not content with that, in 1958, he wrote and published a book entitled *Admiralty Brief.* This attracted the attention of the Circuit prosecutors. I think his indictment is worth reproducing in full as a fine example of its kind.

Statement of Offence

Blowing a trumpet contrary to Section 2 of the Steam Whistles Act 1872.

Particulars of Offence

Edward Terrell on numerous days between 1st January 1958 and 20th November 1958 by means of a written instrument blew a trumpet knowing the same to be his own without the consent of the local sanitary authority.

I do not know what penalty was imposed by the Junior, but I believe on good authority he never paid it. For all that, he won a famous and unexpected (by everybody except himself) victory over another Oxford circuiteer, Edward Eveleigh Q.C., in the House of Lords, having lost in both lower courts. He was acting for a blind client who had fallen over an obstruction on a pavement in S.E. London.[47] In argument in reply, he cited and relied on the venerable authority of Leviticus, chapter 19 verse 14.[48] I believe that, very laudably, he appeared in both the Court of Appeal and the House of Lords without fee, Legal Aid having been granted only for the trial at first instance.

John Foster Q.C., the Recorder of Oxford in the early 1960's, was a notorious ladies' man. When sitting in the Town Hall Court, he used to bring his women friends, ostentatiously dressed, to sit with him on the Bench (on some occasions two of them at once, one on each side) whence they could, and did, watch him with admiration, and also, no doubt, each other with interest. In consequence, he was once prosecuted for Night Poaching contrary to the (now repealed) Night Poaching Act 1844.

Michael Talbot also had been prosecuted in 1955 as follows:

Statement of Offence

Personation, contrary to the False Personation Act 1874.

Particulars of Offence

Michael Chetwynd Talbot falsely and deceitfully personated a barrister of learning and discretion with intent to obtain a valuable thing, namely the Recordership of Banbury.

Circuit Indictments continued, in a rather attenuated and lukewarm form, during the 30-year transitional existence of the Midland & Oxford Circuit. They were stopped in about 1995 after a certain former Midland circuiteer (recently deceased) took pompous umbrage – and I believe complained to the Leader – when he was quite properly indicted (I think for Indecent

47   see *Haley v. London Electricity Board* [1965] A.C. 778.

48   'Thou shalt not curse the deaf, nor put a stumbling block before the blind'. see page 788.

Exposure) for having caused or permitted his house and garden to be visited by and depicted in the pages of, not *House and Garden*, which might have been glossily acceptable, but the rather down-market *Homes & Gardens*.

We have also lost the very close personal relationship between Bench and Bar, which derived from a mostly part-time judiciary at Quarter Sessions. When Brian Gibbens was sitting as Recorder of Oxford, the Bar used to travel with him to and from Oxford by train. We had breakfast of boiled eggs and toast together on the 8.05 from Paddington, and on the return journey, tea as far as Didcot, and thereafter whisky and soda, or gin and tonic. It made for a good, and efficient, working relationship in Court, and was much more pleasant than the wearisome car journey on the A40, precursor of the M40.

We have also lost the generous hospitality of the City of Oxford which used to provide a handsome lunch, and also afternoon tea if the day's sitting lasted so long, for everyone in Court (except the jury and the accused persons) on *every* day of the City Sessions' sitting[49]. We were summoned to the lunch table from sherry in the Mayor's Parlour by the stentorian voice of the City Mace Bearer, Mr. Leslie Boddy, (also recently deceased) intoning:

'Mr Mayor, Mr Recorder, Ladies and Gentlemen, luncheon awaits your pleasure'.[50]

Nowadays you have to pay for a half-baked potato in the Court canteen.

The last, and perhaps most serious, loss, is the use for their intended purpose of many, maybe hundreds over the whole country, of court-rooms and court-houses. The Beeching Report was justifiably severe (and quite amusing) in its condemnation

---

49 Many other Borough Sessions extended hospitality to the Bar, but only on the first working day.

50 I am indebted to His Honour Peter Crawford Q.C. for this valuable recollection.

of the facilities at many Courts. In a wholly accurate passage, much-quoted in the Press, they wrote, in para 109:

> *'Accused persons, litigants, witnesses, jurors, police officers and even solicitors and counsel conferring with clients, all jostle together in embarrassing proximity in halls and corridors, which far from providing any elements of comfort, may well be stacked with the paraphernalia associated with other uses of the building such as dismantled staging, parts of a boxing ring, or the music stands for a brass band contest ... Behind the scenes, the judge's retiring room may be not much bigger than a cupboard,*[51] *and may indeed serve the char-women in that capacity when its distinguished occupant is gone'.*

The pre-1972 Court buildings – a few of which are still in use – dated from virtually every period of English and Welsh history, and architecture, since the Norman Conquest. The oldest I ever sat in as Recorder, and appeared at as counsel, was in Leicester Castle, which Prof. Pevsner says is Norman – or maybe even Saxon: a moving experience. But the judicial lavatory there was the smallest I have ever seen, or used. It was rather worryingly positioned directly over the River Soar. Other interesting buildings were at Derby (Commonwealth), Stafford (Georgian) and Birmingham (magnificent Victorian Tudor, now used by the City Magistrates). The delightful Gothick Courts in Lincoln Castle were, I believe, saved from abandonment only by the personal intervention of the then Lord Chief Justice, Lord Lane, a Midland circuiteer.

The important features of these old Courts were that they were all different from each other, and also, less tangibly, that their age and design gave them dignity and gravitas. Nowadays

---

51   Sir Frank MacKinnon *op cit* p.65 described the facilities at Beaumaris as follows: 'I retired to the "Judge's Room". This was a small wooden cupboard, in which there was just room for me to sit on a Windsor chair and ... to smoke a pipe'. The Court is now open to the public and well worth visiting, but smoking is prohibited!

we are told that accused persons – particularly young ones – are intimidated by the old-fashioned Courts. A possible view is that a measure of intimidation is not necessarily undesirable, and may even be conducive to veracity. An amiably reactionary and choleric Circuit Judge in the East Midlands said to me, with some vigour, that if a Court looks – as many of them now do – like a coffee or wine bar, it will be treated as such by its customers. The modern Crown Court obviously derives from a reach-me-down, Civil Service kit, with a Royal coat of arms made of expanded polystyrene, and has a dismal sameness about it, from one end of the country to the other. There are also some choice euphemisms on display. The cells are nowadays 'The Custody Suite', with all that that implies. I am sorry to have to report that the same 'Standard Issue Court Kit' has been used for the new Courts in the East Wing of the Law Courts in the Strand. G.E.Street, who won the competition to design the main building in 1888, must be turning in the grave in Westminster Abbey to which the job prematurely despatched him.

A linked problem is to find a worthy use for these buildings left behind by the tide of modernisation. At Oxford I was pleased to find recently that the two Courts in the County Hall were substantially unchanged: the fine Assize Court still used by the Coroner, and the Council Chamber (which had been equipped and used as a second court) still in use by the Council: on my visit it was about to house the new Citizenship ceremony. But the Town Hall's panelled Court (scene of John Cleese's, and a lot of my, advocacy)[52] does not seem to have found any new use, save the ignoble one of use as a film set for the implausible Judge Deed. The benches are now furnished with William Morris cushions, but it has a sad, abandoned feel to it. The upstairs Court[53] has been taken over by the City's accountants – they are welcome to it! All too many of the other former Courts have been turned into unvisited museums.

---

52   see pages 3 & 9 above.

53   pages 20 & 21 above.

Oxford Assize Court
(photograph by the author)

Memorial outside Oxford Assize Court
(photograph by the author)

Oxford, predictably, provided mildly entertaining stories about its new Courts. The big panelled Court in the Town Hall was used by both the City Quarter Sessions and the City Magistrates. We used to robe – and disrobe – in the Magistrates' Clerk's office, where he and his secretaries put up with us with courtesy, but with diminishing patience. The Magistrates' Clerk was a very charming, but wily, man called White. He obtained funds from the City Fathers to build a new Magistrates' Court in St. Ebbe's for their sole use. The architect was instructed (so Mr. White told me) to build the Court rooms of such a size that a jury box could never be squeezed in, thus forestalling any further attempt by a superior Court to take over 'his' Court. In this he has been successful, so far.

But the Lord Chancellor's Department (not known for great expertise in property matters) had problems after 1971 in finding urgently-needed new premises for the Oxford Crown Courts. They thought they had found what they wanted on the west side of St. Aldates', just north of Folly Bridge and opposite the Police Station. When they applied for planning permission to revamp the building, including its street frontage, they discovered that it had been the first City Centre showroom of Morris Motors[54], and was therefore (in its way) an important part of Oxford's 20th century history. The facade had to be, and has been, preserved. The Courts inside are the usual characterless rooms with nothing, except Judge Mynett's portrait, to distinguish them from dozens of others. By a strange coincidence, in the same Court there is a huge Victorian double portrait of Lord Brougham, looking rather weather-beaten,[55] and a visiting French jurist.

I ought to mention here something that the visiting High Court (or 'red') judges have lost at Oxford: their lodgings in St. Giles'. Towards the Northern end of that fine street, and on the

---

54   Sir Frank MacKinnon op. cit. p.252 tells of his discovery that the boy who used to pump up his bicycle tyres, when he (F.M.) was an undergraduate, went on to become Lord Nuffield.

55   see page 18 above.

East side, is an elegant Georgian building (No. 16) which, like many Georgian buildings in central Oxford, belongs to St. John's College (incidentally the landlords of my chambers premises in Beaumont Street). The St. Giles' building was originally the town house of the Dukes of Marlborough, and thereafter, for many years, the Assize judge's lodgings. Sir Frank MacKinnon describes the house in detail, and his enjoyment of it, in *On Circuit*;[56] his following pages are full of obscure and quaint learning about Oxford and its ceremonies. It was an easy journey for the judge to travel, by large chauffeur-driven car, to St. Giles for lunch and to return to the Assize Court in New Road for the afternoon session.

However in the mid-60s, pre-Beeching, St. John's announced that it wanted to have the full-time use of this building for its own purposes, so the visiting Judge(s) had to be found somewhere else to stay. Rooms were found at Shotover Park, a stately 18th century pile belonging to Sir John Miller (very recently deceased),the Master of the Horse, a few miles east of Headington on the approach to Oxford from London, through the intermediacy of Mr Justice Stable (known to everyone as 'Owlie') and a great favourite on the Oxford Circuit: he took his dogs with him to inspect the House and said if they liked it (as they did) it would do for the judges[57].

The problem with Shotover was that it was too far outside Oxford for the Judge to get back there easily for lunch and return to the Court by 2.15. So arrangements were made for the Judge to have his lunch not, as you might expect with other slightly lower forms of judicial life, but with the Head of one or other of the colleges. The red judge would quite often invite the barristers in the case in front of him to join him for lunch. This arrangement was not always a success with all those involved.

---

56   at page 175.

57   I am indebted to His Honour Harold Wilson for this. Owlie Stable's dogs were presumably not as alarmed as I was by the huge stuffed bear standing in the Hall, holding a ragged staff.

I well remember being asked by the Assize judge, Sir Gilbert Paull, with my opponent, to have lunch at Christ Church with the Dean (the Head of that college and also the Dean of the Cathedral). Paull J. had had a massive practice when at the Bar, but he was a too-talkative, and hence a difficult, judge. The lunch was a painful and embarrassing occasion. Dean Simpson, the mildest and most courteous of men, obviously found the judge tiresome (as indeed he was). We were constrained to listen to and laugh politely at an unbreakable string of well-worn anecdotes and reminiscences from Sir Gilbert, who clearly regarded himself as the host, and not the guest, of the Dean. We were all (except the Judge) glad to get back to Court. Possibly as a result of incidents like that, Sir Michael Davies tells me that he had to be content with sandwiches in his room at Court.[58]

I can easily share the scepticism of the assertion, advanced to Lord Beeching and his colleagues, that the old forms and ceremonies with trumpeters and javelin men had a salutary and deterrent effect on the criminal classes. But the loss of the impressive buildings and rooms in which cases were actually heard has, I believe, had a devaluing effect on the administration of criminal justice.

Against these losses there ought to be set off the advantages that Oxford circuiteers had, from 1972 onwards, in having access, both as counsel and as Recorders, to what had formerly been exclusively Midland Circuit territory. I sat for many years as a Recorder in the East Midlands and Lincolnshire, making the pleasant acquaintance of the local Bars and judiciary: and I also appeared as counsel in the same area, receiving perfect courtesy and affability from Midland circuiteers. So it was not all bad news.

---

58 A lavishly illustrated book, called *Silence in Court*, devoted to this sad topic was published in 2004 by English Heritage and others. On page 83 is a heart-breaking photograph of the fine old Court at Derby overgrown by a jungle of invading Buddleia, and on pages 98 and 99 are a good picture and written account of the Court in Leicester Castle (see page 41 above).

Chapter 6

Lord Campbell's Insult Refuted

On 11th March 1810 John Campbell, the future Chief Justice of the Queen's Bench (1850 to 1859) and Lord Chancellor (1859 to his death in 1861), wrote a letter to his father from Worcester. Two days later he added a postscript :

> 'The Oxford circuiteers are accomplished gentlemen, but no lawyers'.[59]

He had joined the Oxford Circuit, having made little progress (or money) in and around London on the Home Circuit, in the previous four years since his call to the Bar. It proved to be a good move: by 1816 he was earning 'very little less than 3,000L a year'[60]. His subsequent colourful career is entertainingly described in his notoriously inaccurate autobiography ('edited' by his daughter), and more reliably in Volume 2 of J.B. Atlay's *The Victorian Chancellors*.

In this chapter I hope to show that the first part of Lord Campbell's assessment remained accurate in both respects in the intervening years, but that his stricture on the legal prowess of Oxford circuiteers is, and has for many years been, unwarranted, whatever may have been their qualities in 1810. Those I mention below are those not yet introduced to the reader, and also those not involved in the Reading Juke-Box Case (see Appendix II below).

First, the lawyers. It has by no means always been the case that appointment to the Bench was an indication of legal ability. There have been Lords Chancellor for whom ties of political, or even family, allegiance alone led to judicial appointment, and in the not-so-distant past either. Mr. Justice (later Lord) Darling, appointed by Lord Chancellor Halsbury in 1897, is often cited

---

59   *Life* Vol 1 page 244.

60   Ibid. page 336.

as an extreme example of a recipient of judicial office which he did not deserve, save on political grounds. His appointment was greeted with widespread public and professional indignation. I regret to say that he (Darling) was an Oxford circuiteer as well as a political time-server. He wrote and had published in 1904 an embarrassing book of verse entitled (alas) *On the Oxford Circuit.* It is said that the law relating to Contempt of Court had to be judicially extended to enable it to penalise the wonderful attack upon him in the *Birmingham Daily Argus* in March 1900, which after much well-deserved abuse concludes:

> '*No newspaper can exist except on its merits – a condition from which the Bench, happily for Mr. Justice Darling, is exempt ... One is almost sorry that the Lord Chancellor had not another relative to provide for on the day that he selected a new judge from among the Larrikins of the law. One of Mr. Justice Darling's biographers states that "an eccentric relative left him much money". That misguided testator spoiled a successful bus conductor'.*

For the full, gloriously insulting, text see *R. v. Gray* (1900) 82 L.T. 534 and Sir Robert Megarry's (first) Miscellany at Law (1955) page 23. The author was fined £100 with £25 costs: a bargain, even at 1900 prices. Darling's shocking behaviour at the Armstrong trial in 1922 outraged even the tolerance of Sir Reginald Bosanquet.[61]

Fortunately those days of *judicial* cronyism have gone. I believe Lord Campbell's gibe "no lawyers" can now be refuted, briefly and conclusively, by enumerating the appointments to the High Court Bench from those who had been Oxford circuiteers before 1972. I reckon that 20 such appointments[62] were made

---

61   op.cit.p.107.

62   In alphabetical order, **Baker (George)**, **Brown (Simon)***, **Brown (Stephen)**, Curtis, Cusack, **Eveleigh**, **Goff (Robert)***, Jones, **Latham**, Neill, **Orr**, Popplewell, **Sachs**, **Saville***, **Scott Baker** (son of George), Slynn*, Stuart-White, Tucker, Wood and **Woolf***.

between 1954 and 1993 from a membership varying between 200 and 250; three had been promoted from the Circuit Bench. Moreover of the 20, no fewer than 12 were promoted to the Court of Appeal – a very high proportion. Those 12 are in bold type in the footnote.

Further promotion to the House of Lords has been bestowed on 5 (asterisked), one of whom (Lord Slynn) got there without bothering to stop at the Court of Appeal on the way. The Circuit provided two Presidents of the Family Division, the first from 1971 to 1979, Sir George Baker, who had been a puisne[63] in the old Probate, Divorce & Admiralty Division since 1961, and presided over its transformation into the Family Division. Later Sir Stephen Brown, who had been a Lord Justice of Appeal from 1983 to 1988, was President from 1988 to 1999.

But the prize for judicial distinction and versatility must go to Lord (Harry) Woolf. His career, after distinction at the Bar, including some years as an Oxford circuiteer and culminating in the post of First Treasury Junior Counsel (Common Law) 1974-79, then proceeded as follows:

High Court Judge 1979-86

Lord Justice of Appeal 1986-92

Lord of Appeal in Ordinary 1992-96

Master of the Rolls 1996-2000

Lord Chief Justice 2000-2005.

A record surely unique thus far, which may yet be equalled by his successor (Lord Phillips), but can hardly be surpassed. His reforms of civil procedure are of lasting importance and benefit.

Faced with those names, facts and figures, I do not think that a modern Lord Campbell (certainly none of the three present holders of that title) could contend that the Oxford circuiteers were "no lawyers".

---

63   See footnote on page 66 note 66 below.

I can personally vouch for the fact that every one of them (and I have at least professional, if not also personal, acquaintanceship with all 20) is, or was, also an "accomplished gentleman". There are however four others, who did not reach the High Court Bench, who must be included in any account of the accomplished gentlemen of the Oxford Circuit during, and shortly after, its last years of independent existence. They are Stephen Tumim, James Irvine, Frank White and Claude Duveen. I am aware that the last of these was, when at the Bar, a Midland circuiteer and hence may be strictly a trespasser in these pages. But he played such a conspicuous part in the professional life of the London end of the Circuit that I think he must be included.

Stephen Tumim was an Oxford circuiteer by birth. His father, Joseph, had been the Clerk of Assize just before my time. Stephen had a large civil, divorce and criminal practice on the Circuit and in London. I appeared with him and against him on many occasions, in and around Oxford. He was a very persuasive advocate, with an amusing drawl in his speaking voice. Whilst Sir John May was the presiding judge of the Midland and Oxford

HH Judge Stephen Tumim, looking relaxed
(by courtesy of Lady Tumim)

Circuit (1973-77), he so far agreed with Lord Campbell that he absurdly declined to approve the appointment of *any* Circuit judges on the Circuit, with chaotic consequences. Shortly after he left that post, about a dozen appointments were made at once in 1978, all very successful: one of them was Stephen Tumim. He sat at Willesden County Court and dealt with his lists there so efficiently that he was usually able to take his lunch at either the Garrick or the Beefsteak Club. His membership of the latter, of which the then Home Secretary, Douglas Hurd, was also a member, led to the brilliant decision to appoint Stephen in 1987 to the post of Chief Inspector of H.M. Prisons. This job had previously been almost unknown to the public and the media. Stephen quickly saw to it that the deplorable state of many prisons was widely publicized and in due course largely remedied. He set himself, and achieved, the objective of abolishing the revolting practice of 'slopping-out', by providing W.C.s in the cells. With great skill and discretion he accomplished in a few years what previous holders of his office had failed to achieve. To his surprise he became a minor celebrity in the process. His appearances on television news programmes, complete with erratic bow-tie and self-deprecating demeanour, brought him to serious and high-powered attention, culminating in an appearance on Desert Island Discs. He conducted a number of special inquiries into prison problems, including (with Harry Woolf) the Strangeways riots in Manchester, and, in more agreeable surroundings, the prison in the Cayman Islands.

For his pains, he was regarded as a 'soft target' by the I.R.A. and as a result he, and his stoical wife Winifred, had immediately and permanently to leave their beautiful Thameside house, containing their admirable picture collection, at Chiswick, and live for months with an armed escort, while camping out in a T.A. barracks in North London. He eventually fell out with the Home Office, and in 1995 his contract was not renewed. But his place in the history of the reform of English prisons is secure and honourable. He was knighted in 1996. He died suddenly in 2003.

HH Judge James Irvine, looking friendly
(by courtesy of Oxford Crown Court)

James Irvine was a delightfully urbane advocate. He had a busy practice on the circuit, and there was general approval and rejoicing when he was appointed to the Circuit Bench in 1972. Wherever he sat, at first in Leicester and later in Oxford, he recorded his precursors by making and exhibiting collections of photographs of former judges of those Courts. At Oxford's Court he organized also the display in the Court corridor of the coats of arms of the High Sherriffs of the county. He often reminded litigants of the fate of the Kilkenny cats, who fought each other until both were dead. The affection in which he was held at the Bar and the Bench was shown by the huge gathering in Merton College Hall for the memorable dinner to mark his retirement. He, of all people, ought to have written this book, but could not be persuaded to do it.

Frank White also had a busy practice on the Circuit, and was a tough but pleasant opponent, with a lively sense of humour. He was one of the Deputy Chairmen of Berkshire Quarter Sessions and I well remember that, when I appeared in front of him in December 1971, in the very last case to be tried at that Court before the Courts Act axe fell, he (typically) had certificates prepared for each member of the jury to commemorate their unique distinction. He really came into his own when, having been appointed to the Circuit Bench in 1974, he was in 1994 promoted to the post of Senior Circuit Judge and put in charge of the new Central London County Court (an amalgamation of the Westminster, Bloomsbury and Marylebone Courts) in Park Crescent, adjoining Regents Park. He there created a strikingly successful judicial organisation, where none had been before. He was deservedly knighted in 1997. It was also characteristic of him that he instituted a series of extremely successful annual summer parties for all the Court's judiciary and its regular practitioners, in the gardens in front of the Court, where Pimms with strawberries and cream were served, and cheerful music was played under the plane trees.

Claude Duveen comes last in this very arbitrary selection. Although (as I have said) he had been a member of the Midland Circuit, he was the judge of the County Courts in Berkshire and, first, from 1958, a deputy chairman, and then, from 1966 to its abolition in 1971, the Chairman of Berkshire Quarter Sessions. He was, for those who did not know him, an alarmingly vocal judge who made his opinions of the matter before him, and of the witnesses, conspicuously clear as the case proceeded. As and when he changed his mind (as he often did) he let everyone know by the vigorous wielding of his pen on the pages of his note-book. He usually came to the right conclusion; but sometimes even the winning litigant went away wondering quite what had hit him, or what he had done wrong. He once sent a colleague of mine a courteous, but firm, note (preserved by its recipient, Mr David Ashton, and reproduced on the next page)rebuking him for wearing a pink shirt under his robes, even though he himself used to wear an outrageous bespoke Old Etonian bow-tie, when sitting at Quarter Sessions. He was a nephew of the famous art dealer, and benefactor of art galleries, Lord (Joseph) Duveen:

expansive eccentricity seems to have run in the family. He appears (unrecognizable as a young man) in a family photograph illustrating a recent biography of his uncle. Claude died in office in 1976. The Circuit was a lot less lively without him. .

I hope not to have given offence by either the inclusion of and comments on any of the above, or the exclusion of others. In truth Lord Campbell's description of *all* my former circuit colleagues as "accomplished gentlemen"[64] can hardly be bettered, though I hope also to have shown that at least some of us were lawyers too.

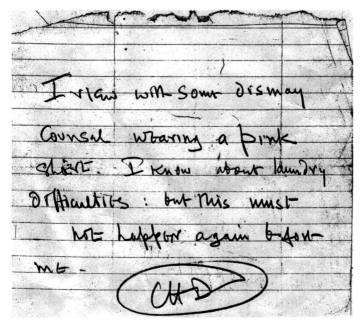

Note from HH Judge Claude Duveen QC to Mr David Ashton
(by courtesy of Mr David Ashton)

---

64   Sir Michael Davies has generously informed me that Oxford and Midland circuiteers were often known respectively as 'the gentlemen' and 'the players': the cricketers who, as amateurs and professionals, first used these appellations were also amalgamated in (I think) the 1960s, and their annual match at Lord's was abolished.

CHAPTER 7

How it is

I embark on this chapter with some hesitation, having been virtually out of practice for about 5 years, though still a member of a busy and expanding civil and criminal set of chambers, with premises in King's Bench Walk in the Temple, and (after a prolonged search) in Beaumont Street in Oxford. However I believe it is worth my making a possibly inaccurate attempt to compare the Bench and the Bar, not just pre- and post-Beeching, but also roughly at one end and the other of my professional career: a period of very great and possibly unprecedented, change. I fear it involves quite a lot of statistics, and the expression of a few heretical opinions.

The Bench

We have already seen how the Beeching reforms introduced a new form of judicial life, the Circuit Judge. In 1962 there were 76 county court judges and about 12 other permanent judges at the Old Bailey and elsewhere. They all became Circuit Judges on 1st January 1972. In 1972/3, just after the Courts Act came into force, there were 140 Circuit Judges. In 2005 there were 611 Circuit Judges[65].

The numbers of High Court and Appeal Court Judges have also increased substantially. In 1962 there were 12 Lords Justice of Appeal (including Lord Denning MR) and 7 Judges of the Chancery Division, 28 of the Queen's Bench, and 11 of the Probate, Divorce & Admiralty Division, that is 46 judges of first instance[66]. In 2006 the comparative figures are as follows: 43 Lords Justices of Appeal (including Lord Phillips CJ), 18

---

65   Yes really! But I may have lost count after about 550.

66   These judges are technically known as 'puisnes' (surprisingly pronounced 'punies'), a word derived from the Latin, via old French, meaning 'junior'.

Chancery Judges, 72 Queen's Bench Judges and 20 Family Judges: that is 110 judges of first instance.

The explanations, if any are needed, for this remarkable rise in the full-time judiciary, lie not only in the continuing increase in criminal work and in the length of trials (referred to in Chapter 2 above), but also in the quantity of legislation Parliament has enacted in the last 50 years. Whole new areas of litigation have been created, in particular in numerous tribunals, from which appeals lie to other, higher, tribunals and thence to the High Court, and beyond to the Court of Appeal.

A recent change which would, I think, have surprised Sir Ronald Bosanquet, is the acquisition by nine members of the Court of Appeal of novel titles, some additional to existing Offices, others wholly new. Thus the Lord Chief Justice is now also the 'President of the Courts of England and Wales' and the Master of the Rolls is the 'Head of Civil Justice'; there are now Vice-Presidents of the Civil Division, of the Criminal Division, and of the Queen's Bench Division as well, not to mention the 'Senior Presiding Judge of England and Wales.' The temptation to say, with W.S.Gilbert, that 'every Lord Justice is somebodee' must be resisted, because there are still 34 of them without any extra appellation.

Another important respect in which the judiciary of today differs from that of 40 or 50 years ago is the existence now of the Judicial Career Structure. Up to the '70s, the only promotion was from the High Court to the Court of Appeal and (for the super elite) to the House of Lords. In those days the Appeal Court salaries were the same as the High Court: the only perquisite was becoming a Privy Counsellor, and hence Right Honourable. Promotion from the county to the High Court was rare[67] and from stipendiary magistrate to the County Court even rarer.

The introduction of the rank of Circuit judge (between the County Court and the High Court) has provided an intermediate

---

67   see page 39 above.

judicial step. The proliferation of 'new' Recorders – a post for which solicitors have since 1972 been eligible – has given another point of entry into the judicial system. It thus has become possible for a solicitor, who has judicial aspirations (and tolerant partners), to become a deputy and then a full-time stipendiary (now called a District Judge), then a Recorder, then a Circuit Judge, then a High Court Judge, and then (who knows?) a member of the Court of Appeal and the Lords. This had always been theoretically possible; but the Beeching changes have made it much more of a practical prospect. With them has come that dangerous and unattractive person, the ambitious judge, whose decisions may be thought to be career-motivated.

The Bar

It is difficult to know where to begin in describing how the Bar has changed in my professional lifetime. Contrary to many forecasts, the numbers of those wanting to start independent practice has risen and continues to rise, but perhaps now less steeply. There are now far more women coming to the Bar than ever before. I think the ratio of the sexes amongst those starting practice is about 50/50: a very welcome development. Sets of chambers have themselves increased in number, and in size, beyond anything remotely contemplated in the 1960's. The location of sets of chambers has changed radically.

In the early 1960's all the sets of barristers' chambers were in one or other of the four Inns of Court in London, apart of course from those in the big provincial cities. In about 1966 Lord Gifford QC (a left-wing barrister peer) shook the establishment to its foundations by opening a set in Covent Garden: contrary to widespread expectation, the world did not come to an end overnight. In the 1980s, my own chambers, when my precursor Peter Crawford QC was Head, were at first refused, but later granted, by the Circuit permission to open the first annexe in Oxford in recent years. There are now two others.

The spread of barristers' chambers from the Inns of Court to the surrounding areas of Central London (the Strand, Fleet Street, the streets off Chancery Lane and, for the very prosperous, Lincoln's Inn Fields) can be seen as the result of a number of factors, the first of which is of course the huge increase in the numbers of persons in practice. The Inns have been very active in creating more space for chambers. In the immediate post-war years there were many solicitors', accountants' and even architects', offices in the Temple; but they have been driven out. Moreover the Inns have, laudably, acquired new premises. The Middle Temple, of which my wife is a Bencher, has expanded westwards into Essex Street where several large sets are now established; and my Inn, the Inner Temple, has very recently taken the bold and historic step of acquiring Serjeant's Inn, an early 20th century group of buildings fronting on to Fleet Street. It stands on the site of the old Serjeant's Inn, to which barristers used to be admitted on becoming Serjeants-at-law (a senior rank abolished in the late 19th century, with controversial consequences for the Bar, but surviving longer in Ireland).

But even these acquisitions have not proved enough to house the Bar. It should also be recalled that many of the buildings in the Inns, destroyed by the Luftwaffe in WWII, were not replaced. In particular Lamb Building used to stand in the middle of Church Court between the Temple Church and Inner Temple Hall: the name is now attached to a post-war building facing Middle Temple Lane. Between the *present* Lamb Building and the West end of Inner Temple Hall were several cramped buildings (Elm Court and Fig Tree Court), which it was obviously right not to rebuild. There was also a building (not rebuilt) standing in the middle of what is now the Middle Temple car park. That is why there are two names, Brick Court and Essex Court, for buildings facing on to what is now one space. Middle Temple Library was, pre-Blitz, where Queen Elizabeth Building now stands, but it is now in Middle Temple Lane.

In the '60s there was much controversy about a very prosperous commercial and shipping set in Essex Court in the Temple, where a lot of forensic intellectual talent congregated. There were, I think, two QCs in the set, and perhaps 7 or 8 busy and able juniors. They had a near monopoly of their very remunerative field of practice. One or two of the juniors applied to the Lord Chancellor for silk, that is to become a QC Lord Chancellor Kilmuir told the applicants and the Head of the Chambers that he would grant the applicants silk, if (but only if) the set split in two in order to 'break the monopoly'. They did so, and the juniors became QCs accordingly. At the time, it was regarded as inappropriate for a set of chambers to have more than two silks on its strength. Nowadays there are several sets of chambers with 12 or more silks and, in addition, over 100 juniors, with a frequently changing membership. I don't know how a Head of Chambers can cultivate any *espirit de corps* amongst such numbers: I guess he can't.

At the other extreme, there are small groups of barristers practising in such surprising places as Mitcham and New Malden, in the suburbs of London.

Modern information technology has of course made it possible to work from home, with access to the law reports on the internet. This, coupled with Mayor Livingstone's Congestion Charge, has resulted in there being almost always space to park a car in the Temple. The convention whereby a silk had to practise out of a London set of chambers has long since been abrogated. There are now very large provincial sets with numerous silks, as there are in London.

Individual barristers, and sets of chambers, have also become much more specialised, with consequences both desirable and the reverse. The ever-increasing complexity of the law, and the growth of new areas of litigation, have made specialisation almost inevitable, at least into broad categories of work, such as crime, family, landlord and tenant, employment and so on. The abolition, in the 1960s, of the Bar's immunity from claims for negligence, and the consequent necessity for insurance against such claims, have strongly encouraged such specialisation. But it can go, and in my opinion has gone, too far – on 'political' or professedly conscientious grounds. There are now barristers, and chambers, who will undertake only defence work in crime, or appear only for tenants and employees, but not for landlords or employers. I deplore this development, and not only on grounds of non-compliance with the 'cab-rank' principle (Rule 601 of the Bar's *Code of Conduct*). You are likely to be a more effective criminal defender, if you have had experience of the problems of prosecuting, and, of course, vice versa.

Another change, in some ways more fundamental than mere numbers, is more difficult to describe. It can perhaps be encapsulated in the expression The Cult of Chambers. In the early 1960s the printed directory of the Bar, then called the *Law List*, indicated the name of each barrister, his or her date of call and professional address and telephone number (no fax or email then). But it did *not* show to which set of chambers the individual belonged. Then, as now, there were addresses (in Crown Office Row and Harcourt Buildings in the Temple in particular) where several different sets of chambers were located; and one or two of them might be more successful than the others. If you wanted to find out of which chambers Mr John Smith was a member, you had to ask him or, if you felt that inappropriate, to go and look at the list at the entrance to the building.

Nowadays and more sensibly, the various directories list the sets of chambers, their members and their main areas of practice. Moreover many sets of chambers have given themselves titles, not simply relating to their location or the Head of Chambers for the time being. Resounding names such as Blackstone, Wilberforce and (more recently) Hailsham and Matrix have been adopted by some sets of chambers, hoping thereby to add lustre to their image. Chambers nowadays list their 'new acquisitions' of glamorous tenants (with their provenance, and sometimes even with photographs as well!) at length in the professional journals.

I think I must include, with regret, a change for the worse in that in recent years the conversation in Court Robing Rooms is almost always about the gross inadequacy of fees for publically-funded work. Thirty or so years ago such fees, while not over-generous, at least bore some reasonable relationship to the work done, to the barrister's seniority and even to his expense in getting to Court; and the conversation in the Robing Rooms could concentrate on more entertaining topics, such as latest Temple gossip or scandal. No longer. The Treasury, at whose parsimonious behest these fees are fixed, and regularly reduced, seems to be determined to drive much of the Criminal Bar out of existence, and to substitute 'district attorneys' to prosecute, and 'public defenders' to defend, in the Crown Court, on the U.S.A. model; an infinitely depressing prospect.

Two other changes have taken place, both of them in my opinion of doubtful value. The first is the Chambers Brochure. In (I think) the mid '70s some second-rate set of chambers thought it could improve its rating by producing a brochure, describing (and depicting in photographs) the chambers, its location, its facilities, its members and the nature of their practices. Anyone with a few weeks' experience of the Bar and some elementary knowledge of human nature could (and I did) easily foresee the scope for pretension, exaggeration, half-truth and dispute that is bound to be inherent in this baleful document. Smith will wish to describe himself in the brochure as an expert in liquor and betting-shop licensing – a lucrative field – but Jones will protest that the only licensing cases Smith has done in the last five years have all been his (Jones') returns and Smith has lost all of them: Smith will retort that Jones always returns his likely losers. A set of chambers will wish to describe itself as (for fictitious example), '*the* leading set dealing with prisoners' rights ': another set will protest that it does at least as much prison work as the other, and has more barristers working in that field. The first set was (it really was) required to reprint the brochure, to delete 'the', and substitute 'a'. Huge sums of money have been spent on brochures, and on their 21st century equivalents, websites: I doubt whether any more work has been procured as a result. But once one set of chambers has one, others with work in the same field must be strong-minded not to follow suit.

The other change of doubtful benefit is the invention of the chambers manager/director/chief executive. Traditionally a set of chambers had a clerk, who was paid a percentage of the barristers' income, a 'boy', and a typist. When I came to the Bar we were paid in guineas (abbreviated to 'guas') but if your fee was, as most of mine were, the irreducible minimum of 2 guas, your solicitor did not pay you £2, 2 shillings (a guinea was 21 shillings, or 105p), but £2, 4 shillings and sixpence (that is £2.22½p). Your clerk got the 4 shillings and the sixpence, and you got the £2. Don't ask me why![68]

When the currency was decimalised, guineas disappeared and so did the 'extra' 2 shillings and sixpence. The minimum fee became £2, so you lost not just 'the shillings in the guineas', but also the 10½p as well. You still had to pay your clerk 10% of £2. So the barrister ended up worse off by 20p, and the clerk by 22½p. There are now very many different ways in which barristers' clerks' remuneration is calculated; and the new, very large sets have a 'team' of clerks, to deal with separate areas of the chambers' work, which is done by a 'team' of barristers in the chambers.

As sets of chambers got bigger and bigger, and the aggregated incomes reached £1 million, then £2 million, etc., etc., some chambers considered that they ought to be run by a person with more experience of business than having been a barristers' clerk for 25 or more years. They consulted head-hunters, who, for a large fee, produced a small list of ex-businessmen and -women looking for a career change. Sometimes these people understood what the Bar was about and were successful, more often they didn't and weren't. Presumably attributable to chambers' managers are such vulgar excesses as inscribed chambers' umbrellas, which

---

68   There is an explanation, but it is too nonsensical to relate.

members are no doubt expected to use around the Temple in wet weather, but which recent prolonged droughts have rendered an even sillier idea.

My own chambers, whilst I was Head, spent thousands of pounds in:

(a)   creating a new space for the director to work in, and then

(b)   choosing her, and then

(c)   getting rid of her, and then

(d)   choosing her successor, and then

(e)   getting rid of him, and then

(f)   rearranging the furniture and the computer terminals, having decided not to replace him.

We are now getting on very well with an excellent team of (mostly male) 'old-fashioned' clerks and receptionists in London and (mostly female) administrators, clerks and typists in Oxford.

Pupillage (the mandatory 12-month period of professional apprenticeship) has also changed beyond recognition. In 1959 I had to pay 100 guineas (£105), furnished by a generous scholarship from the Inner Temple, to my pupil-master, Douglas Lowe, who had distinguished himself in his youth by winning the 800 metres Gold Medal at two consecutive Olympic Games in the '20s; and (I think) £10 to his clerk. Nowadays it is compulsory for sets of chambers to pay, or at least guarantee, £10,000 to any twelve-month pupil they take on. Prosperous and high-powered chambers will pay much more to promising young men and women. Chambers, and the Inns of Court, carry out elaborate selection procedures for prospective pupils and scholars, and some even set written examinations.

Thank Goodness I never had to undergo them: the old-boy network was quite good enough for me, and (it seems) me for it.

Another (as I think, beneficial) innovation at the Bar of the last thirty or so years is the mini-pupillage, whereby young men and women spend a week or two (often during their university vacations) in a busy set, going to Court, attending conferences, and reading sets of papers in chambers. This has the great advantage of giving young people a taste of practice at the Bar, without commitment or much expense on either side. In my day the only way to find out if you liked it (or it liked you) was to qualify by joining an Inn, eating your compulsory dinners, passing the examinations and getting a formal full-scale pupillage – a lengthy and expensive process, which might prove all in vain. Sometimes the new system is abused by individuals accumulating a pointlessly large number of mini-pupillages or, on one infamous occasion, by so far breaching the security system of the local Crown Court that all the combinations on the locked doors had to be changed. On the whole it is a valuable institution, and has probably encouraged a lot of recruits to the Bar, who might otherwise have thought it was a career out of their reach.

At the other end of a barrister's professional life, great changes have taken place, and are at the time of writing taking place, in connection with appointments to the Bench, and also to the rank of Queen's Counsel. The Lord Chancellor, whose own ancient and historic post at the heart of the English legal system narrowly escaped peremptory abolition on 12th June 2003 by decree of the Prime Minister's then Press Secretary, has divested himself of the duty of making these appointments. Indeed, no new silks have been appointed since the 121 (an unusually large number) sworn in before Lord Chancellor Irvine on 29th April 2003. A wholly new process is now in operation, and 175 fresh appointments were announced in July 2006. It is obviously both premature and inappropriate to comment on these matters here. Even so the 'demography' of the Bar must have been changed for the future by the 3½ year hiatus, during which time appointments, retirements and deaths will have reduced the numbers of silks in practice. Official up-to-date and complete statistics are not available. The most recent are for the year to end of November

2001.There were then 10,334 barristers in independent practice, of whom, 1,078 (roughly 10%) were Queen's Counsel. By December 2004 the total number of the practising Bar had risen to 11,564; the number silks in practice must have fallen, but I do not know by how many.

As it usually is, and probably always will be, the profession is in a state of flux; and the times are interesting.

APPENDIX I

The old Circuit Rules, and

The Oxford/Midland Circuit Disputes

This Appendix will, I fear, be quite hard work for those of less than tenacious disposition, which is why I have put the material in a separate section.

The Circuit Rules did not apply to solicitors, only to barristers. Nor did they did apply to either the Magistrates' Courts (in any of their various jurisdictions) or the County Courts, in both of which solicitors and barristers both had unfettered rights of audience, as did the Bar. The Rules applied only to Assizes and Quarter Sessions.

Most barristers belonged to a Circuit. Some London practitioners, such as Sir Frank MacKinnon,[69] never joined one. But if you wanted to work outside London, in particular to be instructed by prosecuting authorities, you had – and still have – to join the appropriate circuit, and pay its, quite moderate, annual subscription. There was, and is, no great formality about joining, or even changing, your circuit, if you could find a proposer and seconder (often your pupil master); though if you change too often, people may wonder why.

In their most rigid form the Circuit Rules, which I think applied equally to all the Circuits, required a barrister who was asked to appear at Assizes or Quarter Sessions that were not on his Circuit:

(a)   to charge his client a 'special fee' of an extra 50 guineas (100 in the case of a QC) – a not negligible amount at the time, and

(b)   to cause his instructing solicitor to instruct also a junior counsel who *was* a member of the circuit upon which he

---

69   op. cit. page 3.

was 'trespassing', at a moderate (but more than nominal) fee. This was known as a 'Kite' brief.[70]

The objective, of course, was simply to discourage 'trespassing' from one circuit on to another.

These two requirements were, from the public's point of view, entirely unjustifiable financial impositions, and were abolished by the Bar Council in the late '60s. They had produced many absurdities at the margins. Thus Liverpool was Northern, as was Manchester, but Birkenhead and Knutsford were both Wales & Chester. I once had a Kite brief as junior to C.M. Clothier (known to everyone as "Spike"), whom I later got to know better, and hugely to admire, when he joined my first chambers when he took silk in 1965. The case was tried at Stafford Assizes (an Oxford Circuit town), but Spike was a Northern Circuiteer: our lay client was the son of a prominent Liverpool solicitor, charged with causing death by dangerous driving. Spike had no trouble in getting him acquitted, and I learned a lot from seeing a high-powered junior in action; but that did not justify the extra cost to the solicitor/ client – which of course he could easily afford!

The abolition of the special fee and the Kite brief did not entirely end the restrictive Circuit practices, but reduced them so significantly that they became unenforceable and obsolete quite quickly. A 'trespassing' barrister was supposed to pay 'place money' of £5 (or guineas per case, or per day, I forget which) to the Circuit he was trespassing on. For a while some Circuits, including the Oxford, found themselves with an embarrassment of riches, which they spent by making grants to pupils of circuiteers. By the time the Courts Act was in force in 1972 these rules had withered away from non-observance, to non-existence.

---

70   Atlay *op. cit.* page 137 says, in his day 'a kite' is a 'back sheet' of paper with instructions to open the pleadings, after which the counsel has no further *locus standi* in the cause'; but he does not explain the circumstances in which it was used. 'Opening the pleadings' was a curious, and pointless, ceremony, at the start of the trial of a civil action with a jury (see the account of *Bardell v. Pickwick* in *Pickwick Papers*, Chapter 34): it was abolished in the '60s.

The Disputes between the Oxford and the Midland Circuits.

During the mid 20th century, a series of disputes broke out between the Oxford and the Midland Circuits which formed an ironic background to the shotgun marriage into which we were forced in 1972. An afternoon's research amongst the Circuit's papers in the Bodleian Library revealed to me what the underlying reasons for these problems were. In 1883, on Birmingham's promotion to higher local government status, it was also promoted into the itinerary of the Assize Judges on *both* the Oxford and Midland Circuits. This, together with the geographical position of Birmingham in Warwickshire (a Midland circuit county), but close to its boundaries with Staffordshire and Worcestershire (both Oxford Circuit counties), gave rise to the anomalous position whereby barristers from both Circuits had rights of audience at Birmingham Assizes.

Before 1883, the three counties of Warwickshire, Worcestershire and Staffordshire had had Assizes only in their eponymous county towns, and there were Quarter Sessions also in Coventry (Midland), West Bromwich, Warley and Wolverhampton (all Oxford). By 1883, when it was decided to hold Assizes at Birmingham as well as Warwick, the Birmingham conurbation had expanded and encompassed the so-called Black Country, which included parts of all three counties.

By the 1960s the Birmingham local Bar consisted of roughly equal numbers of Oxford and Midland circuiteers.

The **first** dispute, in point of time, seems to have broken out in the early 1930s. It involved the assertion by the Midland Circuit that it had the exclusive right to provide candidates for the (important) post of Recorder of Birmingham. I do not know what the Circuit provenance of previous Recorders of Birmingham had been. In any event the Oxford Circuit disputed the Midland's claim to exclusivity. The course of the matter is set out in a long letter in the Bodleian Library dated 13th April 1954 from Lord

Chancellor Simonds (who I think may have been a former Oxford circuiteer) to George Baker QC, the then leader of the Oxford Circuit (always known as "Scotty").

The letter says that when the dispute emerged, the then Lord Chancellor (probably Sankey) in whose gift the appointment lay, referred the question to the Bar Council. That body decided in December 1931 'by a very large majority' that members of both the Oxford and the Midland Circuits were eligible. The Midland Circuit was dissatisfied with this result and asked the Bar Council to reconsider the issue, on the ground that it had not previously considered all the material evidence. The Bar Council did reconsider it, and in January 1932 came to the very same conclusion as before.

There the matter rested until 1937, when a vacancy in the Recordership arose. The then Lord Chancellor Hailsham[71] consulted the Attorney- and the Solicitor-General, both of whom advised the Lord Chancellor that members of both circuits were eligible. Lord Chancellor (Douglas) Hailsham thereupon offered the post to an Oxford circuiteer – who declined it ! He then offered it to a Midlander, who took it.

Lord Simonds' letter concluded by informing Scotty Baker that he regarded it as his (the Lord Chancellor's) job to appoint the best candidate from whatever circuit, and that members of both circuits, and possibly even of others, were eligible.

Quite right! Judge Peter Crawford QC was the last former Oxford Circuiteer to be the Recorder of Birmingham, and later of Oxford.

The **second** dispute, and one which I remember causing much consternation, involved rights of audience and so-called 'cross-committals'. It sometimes – possibly quite often – happened that an Oxford circuiteer would be instructed to appear at (say) Coventry Magistrates' Court (to which of course the Circuit rules

---

71   Father of the proponent of the Courts Bill, supra.

HH Judge Peter Crawford QC, looking pleased
(by courtesy of Ox ford Crown Court)

did not apply: see above) for (say) William Sikes on a charge
of murdering one Nancy. Mr. Sikes might well be committed
for trial to Birmingham Assizes. In the early 1960s a dispute
broke out as to whether the Oxford circuiteer could 'follow'
the case to, and appear for Sikes at, Birmingham Assizes. The
Midland Circuit said he could not because the case derived from
a Midland circuit county, namely Warwickshire, and the Oxford
circuiteer's rights to appear at Birmingham Assizes related
only to cases deriving from an Oxford circuit county, such as
Staffordshire. The Oxford Circuit said Birmingham Assizes were
open to members of both circuits, irrespective of the source of
the case. This dispute caused acrimony and difficulty, in which

HH Judge King-Hamilton QC, looking percipient
(by courtesy of himself)

the interests of the Circuits were hotly defended and those of Mr.
Sikes were completely ignored.

A complicated series of letters is to be found in the Bodleian
Library, culminating in a letter of 12th February 1964 from
Lord Chancellor Dilhorne to the Circuit's then leader, Alan
King-Hamilton QC, wholly vindicating the Oxford Circuit's
contentions and rejecting the Midland's. Alan had the satisfaction

of announcing this result to great acclaim and rejoicing, at a circuit dinner at Gray's Inn.

Quite right too!

The **third**, and last, dispute (of which I knew nothing at the time) arose in the late '60s, shortly before the Beeching Report. It related to the nominations made by the Attorney-General to prosecute serious criminal cases at Birmingham. The Attorney-General then had the right to nominate prosecuting counsel in such cases: this is now the job of the Director of Public Prosecutions. Again, there was a demarcation dispute as to whether a Midland circuiteer could be, or even had to be, nominated to prosecute a case at Birmingham Assizes deriving from an Oxford Circuit county, and vice versa.

In 1967 the Leaders of the two Circuits (Brian Gibbens and Bernard Caulfield) came to an agreement, endorsed by the Lord Chancellor, that members of each circuit had the right to be nominated to prosecute cases at Birmingham Assizes deriving from their own Circuit counties, and that the Midland had no monopoly.

Quite right again!

Can you wonder that we found it ironical that we should be forced into merger with the Midland? We had had no such problems with our other neighbours. But I believe they did with theirs.

APPENDIX II

The Reading Juke-Box Case

Having disparaged Sir Ronald Bosanquet's book, I propose to follow his example, and conclude with an account of a notable Circuit case, in which I played a minor part. I do so because it was my first case of any substance and, mainly, because it introduced me to many of the Circuit's then luminaries, some, but not all, of whom we have met before.

The case was tried in the early summer of 1964, at the same time as the Great Train Robbers were being tried at Aylesbury. They got all the headlines. Ours was in truth not a newsworthy case involving, as it did, a common enough kind of fraud, using the device of hire purchase agreements to extract money from finance companies. The only unusual features of the case were that the subject-matter of the deals was not cars, but juke boxes and the customers were, not drivers, but pub licensees. The fraud lay in the fact that many of the juke-boxes were of course fictitious, existing only on paper.

It was tried at Reading Assizes in the second Court, while other cases came and went in the first Court next door, and our judge was Nield J, the promoted first judge of the Manchester Crown Court (see page 18 above). It lasted about 8 weeks. The accused persons fell into two categories: two big fish, and about four smaller fry, of diminishing size and importance. The dramatis personae of the Bar were, to the best of my recollection after over 40 years, as follows:

For the Crown:	Kenneth Mynett QC,
leading	Michael Talbot;
For the first big fish:	Paul Wrightson QC,
leading	John Murchie;
For the second big fish:	Charles Lawson QC,
leading	Christopher Oddie;

For the smaller fry:	Brian Gibbens QC
leading	me
and	Alan King-Hamilton QC,
leading	Aron Owen;
and	Edward Terrell QC
leading	Thomas Whipham
and	Francis Barnes,
leading	Michael Rush.

I was lucky enough to get this, very desirable, brief (from a well-known firm of Central London solicitors doing criminal work) because a senior junior in my then chambers, with a large Circuit practice, returned it. He thought, wrongly as I think, that being out of general circulation for weeks on end would damage his practice in other Courts. I did not complain.

Most of the Bar travelled together to and from Reading every day by train. When the case began the trains we travelled on were, on most days, hauled by magnificent steam locomotives. As time went on, these were replaced by characterless, evil-smelling and unreliable diesels. Towards the end of the case we looked back with affection on how it had begun 'in the days of steam'. I have already introduced the reader to both the prosecuting counsel and to Messrs. Gibbens and Terrell. I will attempt vignettes of some of the others.

Paul Wrightson was, in appearance, a terrifying figure, but personally absolutely charming. He was tall and skeletally thin (probably from a wasting disease) with a bony, beaky nose, a slight stoop and a theatrically sinister smile. In cross-examination, he attacked the pompous, overfed and evasive witnesses from the finance companies with vigour, wit and sarcasm, and in his closing speech described them as 'so sharp that their clothes will not hang together'. Before he took silk he had had a huge practice before the Queen's Bench Divisional Court, arguing obscure points of law[72] on appeal from Magistrates' Courts. He was the last Recorder of Walsall.

John Murchie, Paul Wrightson's junior, was in every sense a larger than life figure. He was a big man with a huge and generous personality. He had a large junior practice at the London end of the Circuit, and was a Deputy Chairman of Berkshire Quarter Sessions. He richly deserved to get silk, but in their inscrutable wisdom the Lords Chancellor of the day rejected his applications. He was appointed to the Circuit Bench in 1974, and was a very popular and successful judge in Reading, at the Old Bailey and in Cyprus: the Temple Church was absolutely packed at his memorial service.

To be in a case with – or against – John was a rare pleasure. He used to while away the longueurs of boring trials by composing doggerel poems involving the participants in the case. His widow Jennie has very kindly supplied me with a large selection, from which I append a typical specimen, obviously, on internal evidence, about the trial of a 3rd year undergraduate:

Nicholas Nicked

A man may drink and drink and drink
　　And end up in the Oxford clink.
To burgle, and assault a copper –
　　It seems to me is most improper.

The simple issue in this case
　　Is must Dobree now face disgrace?
Though all his conduct must deplore
　　It may still be within our law.

---

72 I seem to recall one involved the question (worthy of A.P. Herbert's Misleading Cases) whether a goldfish was 'an article' within the Sunday Trading legislation.

HH Judge John Murchie, thinking of a rhyme
(by courtesy of Mrs.John Murchie
and Messrs Ede & Ravenscroft)

Did he breach and enter Hall's?[73]
    Why no – the very thought appals
And yet we know he ran away
    'But I was drunk' we've heard him say.

PC Pritchard and PC Reed
    Can no longer run at speed
Soft living in their Panda car
    Means now they never can run far.

Dobree's conduct then got better,
    Apology is sent by letter.
A nice young man, by all he's pitied.
    It would be nice if he's acquitted.

Moral

When you dine at College Club
    Do not then drink in outside pub
If providence looks after fools
    In June you still may take your Schools.

Verdict: Not guilty   28 iv 72

Charles Lawson was another imposing figure. He habitually wore an expression of ill-suppressed amusement, and was blessed with a wonderfully resonant deep voice, which lent authority to even the most implausible assertions of his clients. His practice was, I think, mostly in London, among the fashionable divorces. He was a bon vivant. I doubt if the produce of Burton-on-Trent, of which Borough he was the Recorder, was much to his taste: I guess he preferred fine claret. A student's reading room in the Inner Temple Library is named in his memory. In 1972 he was appointed a permanent Judge at the Old Bailey.

    Christopher Oddie, his junior, had a huge practice in and around Oxford. He had the knack of getting and keeping a jury's

---

73   A posh man's shop in the High.

attention by speaking very quietly, and the closer he got to his best point, the more softly he spoke. It was a very subtle and unusual technique, and brought him much success. I remember how welcoming he was when I turned up at Oxford City Quarter Sessions for the first nerve-racking time. Like John Murchie, he should have been granted silk, but was refused. He and his wife gave an excellent party for the judge and the Bar during the case. He became a very popular Circuit Judge in Central London.

Alan King-Hamilton was the Leader of the Circuit at the time of the trial, and of the sharpest of the disputes with the Midland (see Appendix I above). We were lucky to be represented by such a mild but tenacious person, whose soft answers could turn away wrath, but still win the argument – as they did! He was a very popular Circuit Leader, always accessible and courteous. I cannot however resist recounting his greeting to me on some social occasion, long after his retirement, when he was about 90 and I was about 60. Being reminded of my name and having given me a penetrating stare, he said 'Ah yes: I remember you, Williams. You used to be quite good-looking'.

His junior, Aron Owen, was a friendly Welshman from a Jewish background and, I believe, very learned in Jewish law. I remember travelling to and from Reading with him with much pleasure. His and Alan King-Hamilton's client was acquitted at the end of the prosecution's case. Alan went straight from Reading to become a permanent Judge at the Old Bailey, where he sat for nearly 20 years. He was obviously (and rightly) very highly regarded there, and as a result he seemed to be given all the most difficult, controversial and high-profile cases to try. He never put a foot wrong in all those demanding years[74].

---

74 But he made several excellent jokes. Perhaps the best involved a juror who wanted to be excused in order to be with his wife 'who was about to conceive'. 'I think you mean about to be confined' said Alan. 'No sir, she is about to conceive' said the juror. 'Well, whichever it is,' said Alan, granting his application, 'I'm sure you ought to be there'.

The reader already knows quite a lot about Edward Terrell (see pages 35-37 above). But I must add two more anecdotes, of both of which I was a witness. The first occurred at a late stage in the case, when his client was giving evidence-in-chief, that is, was answering questions put to him by Edward himself. One of the most fundamental and elementary rules of a trial is that counsel must not ask leading questions of his own witness, that is, questions which suggest the answer hoped for. The following ensued:

Edward Terrell to his client, grandiloquently:

> Did you have the slightest idea that that document was a forgery when you signed it?

Kenneth Mynett (prosecuting), wearily:

> The question is flagrantly leading, would my friend please refrain from leading his witness?

E.T., rather testily:

> I will rephrase the question. Mr. Smith, when you came to sign this paper, did it ever occur to you that it might not be in order?

K.M., even more wearily:

> My Lord, I'm sorry to have to intervene again, but my learned friend has now asked the same objectionable question twice.

Nield J, long-sufferingly and patiently:

> Mr. Terrell, I think Mr. Mynett has some grounds for complaint, even against so senior a counsel as yourself.

E.T.,graciously, even obsequiously:

> My Lord, I apologise: I will try again. Now then Mr. Smith, you heard what my Lord said. So next time I ask you a leading question, please don't answer it.

General mayhem and hilarity. Even Nield J gave a wintry smile.

Even later in the case, while the jury were out considering their verdicts, Edward entertained us in the robing room, which was separated from the jury's room by only a flimsy partition, by trying to demonstrate his skill in sticking a stamp on the ceiling[75]. After several failed attempts he succeeded, to noisy acclaim, whereupon Brian Gibbens raised the stakes by betting Edward he could not hit a moving target, with the words 'Go on Edward, see if you can stick a stamp on that fly's arse'. I am sorry to report that numerous attempts at this all failed. The jury must have wondered what all the laughter was about.

Francis Barnes was a meticulous advocate. His pockets were full of pens and pencils in many colours, and his note book resembled a wiring diagram or the map of the London Underground. He had been one of the prosecuting team at Nuremburg and spoke excellent German. We had a German-speaking witness, who needed an interpreter. Francis vigorously challenged the interpreter's version of an answer to a crucial question, asked, not by himself, but by John Murchie. A lively Anglo-Teutonic dispute broke out, the interpreter being of course insulted that his expertise was coming under attack. Francis was the last Recorder of Warley in the Black Country.

Michael Rush was about the same seniority as me; we were the two junior juniors in the case. He was in the same, strongly Oxford Circuit, chambers as Francis, and became the Circuit Junior for 1966. Having done his National Service in the Grenadier Guards, he had a ferociously 'short back and sides' haircut. He never really prospered at the Bar, went on the Circuit Bench, but died sadly young, in his 50s.

The big fish were convicted and the small fry (perhaps luckily) acquitted.

---

75 For the uninitiated, this is done by placing a stamp, sticky side up, on top of as heavy a coin as possible (in those days half-a-crown was ideal, nowadays a £2 piece would do) and throwing the coin flat up to the ceiling, where you hope the stamp sticks.

This was my introduction to many of the characters of the Bar's Oxford Circuit in action. Within less than 8 years, the Circuit and the Assizes had been abolished, the Crown Court had been moved from its dignified Victorian Courthouse to a decrepit and inaccessible shack on the outskirts of the town, and Reading had become part of the South-Eastern Circuit.

Looking back, more than 40 years later, it still seems a pity; but it was good while it lasted.

INDEX

Abbreviations

AG	Attorney-General
BC	Royal Commission on Assizes and Quarter Sessions 1966-1969
BG	Brian Gibbens QC (later HH)
Ct	Circuit
Cts Act	Courts Act 1971
GW	The author
HH	His Honour (title of County Court and, later, of Circuit Judge)
J	Mr Justice (title of High Court Judge)
KC	King's Counsel
KM	Kenneth Mynett QC (later HH)
LC	Lord Chancellor
LCJ	Lord Chief Justice
LJ	Lord Justice of Appeal
LAO	Lord of Appeal in Ordinary (Law Lord)
Md&Ox Ct	Midland & Oxford Circuit
Md Ct	Midland Circuit
MR	Master of the Rolls
NE Ct	North-Eastern Circuit
Nn Ct	Northern Circuit
Ox Ct	Oxford Circuit
Oxon	Oxfordshire
QC	Queen's Counsel

QS   Quarter Sessions

RB   Lord (Richard) Beeching
RJ-BC   Reading Juke-Box Case (Appendix II)

Salop   Shropshire
S-E Ct   South-Eastern Circuit
SG   Solicitor-General

Wn Ct   Western Circuit
W&CCt   Wales & Chester Circuit

Index

Asterixed entries are to Illustrations.

Abingdon; Its Court of QS abolished 46
    Its railway station abolished 46
    Its Recorders 47
Alexander the Great; Teaches RB a lesson 27
Andrews, J Cartographer of map of Cts 12,13*
Anglesey; GW travels overnight from, to Oxon QS 8
    Name of one of the Welsh Cts 14 note
Appeal, Court of, New Titles in 67
Appleford, a village in Oxon
    Its railway Halt abolished 46
Archbold, Criminal Pleading, Evidence & Practice
    Fitzwalter Butler, its editor 20
    Scoured for offences for Ct Indictments 49
Ashton, David: Rebuked by HH Claude Duveen QC 64/5
Assent, Royal, To Courts Bill, etc 36
Assizes; Abolished, 37
    Defects in, 22/3
    Described, 4/6
    History and origins of, 4/5
Audience, rights of
    Oxford circuiteers, at Birmingham Assizes, 23,80
    Solicitors at QS, and in the Crown Court, 10,36
Aylesbury, Assizes, Great Train Robbers tried at, 84

Bailey, Old see Old Bailey.
Baker, Rt Hon Sir George ('Scotty') 56 note
    J.and President of P,D and A (later Family) Division 60
    Elected Leader of Ox Ct 11 note
    Letter to, from Simmonds LC 80
Baker, Rt Hon Sir Scott, J and LJ
    Son of Scotty,supra. 59 note
Baker, John QC
    Organised sweep-stake at dinner for KM
    On his first mention of Europe 41
Banbury; Its QS abolished 47
    Its Recorder indicted for Personation 50

Jury of 13 discharged at, 47
Bar of England and Wales
        'As it is' 68 seq
        'As it was' before Cts Act 10 seq
        Numbers in practice at, 31
        Numbers of women in practice at, 68
        Specialization, at 70
Bar Council (General Council of the Bar)
        Supplies erroneous figures to BC as
        to numbers in practice in Birmingham 30
Barbados, tiny village in, named Oxford 1
Barnes, Francis; Counsel in the R J-B C 91
        Possessor of multi-coloured pens. 91
        Prosecutor at Nuremburg 91
Beaumaris; Sir Frank MacKinnon's experience of, 52 note
Bedford; An Assize town on Md Ct 14
        Sir Frank MacKinnon unemployed at, 5
Beeching, Lord (Richard) (RB) 24*
        Appointed to chair BC 25
        His career 25, 37
        His conduct of BC 25 seq
        Holds press conference 35
Beeching (Royal) Commission (BC)
        Appointed 26
        Minutes of Meetings of, 26
        Report, drafts 28
        Final 30 seq
Beefsteak Club; Hurd,D. and Tumim,S, both members of, 62
Benson, Stephen
        Distinguished a deduction from an inference 47
        Penultimate Recorder of Abingdon 47
Birmingham
        Assizes, instituted in 1883 79
        Rights of audience at 80
        Eligibility to Recordership of 80
        International Conference Centre at,
        Venue for Md Ct Ball 46
        Local Bar, Ct membership of 30
        Regional Centre selected by BC 32
Black Country; QSs cooperate to avoid clashes, in vain 10

Boddy, Leslie; Oxford City Mace Bearer 51
    His summons to the luncheon table 51
Bodleian Library; Ox Ct archives deposited in, 48, 79
Bosanquet, HH Sir Ronald KC; his book 'The Ox Ct' 2
    Referred to, 67, 84
Brecon; An Assize Town on the W&C Ct 14
    Name of a former Welsh Ct 14
Bristol; A Regional Centre selected by BC 32
    Its Tolzey Court abolished. 30
Brochures, Chambers; Fortunes spent on, 72
    GW's views on 72
    Disputes engendered by, 72
Brock, 'Tommy'
    Discovered by Mr Tod q.v. in Mr Tod's bed 3
    Threw scalding tea all over Mr Tod 3
    Violent fight with Mr Tod 3
Brougham, LC; His character 18
    Introduced Central Criminal Court Act 1834 18
Brown, Rt Hon Sir Stephen 59 note
    J, LJ, and President of the Family Division 60
Brown, Lord (Simon)
    J, LJ, and LAO 59 note
Butler, Fitzwalter
    A Deputy/Assistant Recorder at Oxford City QS 20
    Editor of Archbold q.v. 20

Cambridge; An Assize Town on S-E Ct
    (formerly on Norfolk Ct) 13
Campbell, Alastair, former Press Secretary to
    Tony Blair, purported to abolish LC 25
Campbell, John, LC; His autobiography cited, and refuted 58
Canterbury Tales; Prologue cited 5
Cardiff; A regional centre – just. 32
Carmarthen; An Assize town on the Welsh Ct 14
    Name of a former Welsh Ct 14
Cartwright Sharp, John Michael; Consulted by BC 28
    Replied to BC 28
Chambers, Barristers'
    Brochures, q.v.
    Changes in, since 1960s 68

Described 10
Head of 10
Managers/directors 73 seq
Premises, location of 68-70
Titles, self-bestowed 71
Cheshire; A County on the W& C Ct, formerly on the
    Nn Ct. 13-14
Chester; An Assize town 13-14
    Basil Nield QC, MP for 18
Christ Church, an Oxford College
    GW et al.had painful lunch with Paull J. at, 57
    Ox Ct Grand night dinner at, 46
Circuits of the Judges and the Bar,
    Described, pre-1972 4-6, 10 seq
    Leaders and juniors 11-12
    Reduction from 7 to 6 proposed by BC 32
    Restrictive Rules as to. 77 seq
Clark, Leo (later QC and HH)
    Returned junior brief in R J-B C to GW 85
Clark, Paul (later HH)
    Deposited Ox Ct archives at Bodleian Library 48
    Last Junior of Ox Ct 48
Cleese, John; Usurped GW's place in Oxford QS Court 3, 53
Clerks, Barristers'; Remuneration of 73
Clothier, C.M.('Spike', later QC)
    GW has junior 'kite' brief to 78
Common Prayer, Book of; Cited 19
Cornwall; A county on Wn Ct 14
    Duchess of, marriage at Windsor Guildhall. 21
Court of Appeal, New Titles in 67
Crawford, Peter QC 81*
    GW's precursor as Head of Chambers 68
    Last Ox Ct Recorder of Birmingham 80*
    Last Ox Ct Recorder of Oxford 80
    Opens Chambers annexe in Oxford. 68
Cumberland; A county on the Nn Ct 13
Curtis, Sir Richard (formerly Recorder of
    Birmingham and J) 59 note
Cusack, Sir Ralph (formerly Leader of Ox Ct and J) 59 note

Darling, J (later Lord)
    Author of painful verses 'On the Ox Ct' 59.
    Bad behaviour of, at trial of Armstrong. 2
    Deplorable appointment of, to High Court 59
    Deservedly insulted in Birmingham Daily Argus. 59
Davies, Sir Michael, J.; Cited 45note, 65note
    Joint leader, with BG, of Md & Ox Ct 42
    Leader, pre-1972, of Md Ct 42
Deed, Judge John; Implausible 53
Demmery, Mrs Vera; Assistant secretary to BC 27, 28
    Referred to, 33
Denning, Lord MR; Referred to, 35, 66
De Piro, Alan QC (later HH); Umbrage taken by,
    at being indicted by Md & Ox Ct 50
    (see Gardens,infra)
Derby; A Md Ct Assize Town 14
    Its fine Commonwealth Assize
    Court abandoned and overgrown 47 note
Devonshire; A Wn Ct county 14
Devizes QS, Dorset; Silk hats worn by judiciary at, 9
Didcot; Gin and tonic/whisky and soda drunk after, 51
    Tea drunk before, 51
Dilhorne, Viscount LC; Referred to 35
Director of Public Prosecutions; Referred to 3
Dorset; A Wn Ct county 14
Draycott, Douglas QC ; A Leader of the Md & Ox Ct 44
    His narrow-boat 44
Draycott, Simon QC; Son of Douglas ditto,q.v.supra 44
Durham; A city and county on N-E (formerly Nn) Ct. 13
Duveen, Claude QC HH; An 'accomplished gentleman' 64
    Rebuked David Ashton for colour of DA's shirt 64,65*

Edward I, King of England; Possibly instituted Assizes. 4
Elizabeth II, Queen of England, etc.
    Assents to Courts Bill, etc. 36
Essex; A county (formerly on the Home)
    Now on S-E Ct 13
Eveleigh, Sir Edward, J. and LJ. 7, 59 note
    Defeated in the House of Lords
    By Edward Terrell QC, q.v 49 . .

Falconer,LC; Nearly abolished by Alastair Campbell,q.v. 75
Falstaff, Sir John,
        Unwisely hid in hamper q.v. in Ford's q.v. house 5
Fletcher, Lord
        Contended in House of Lords for solicitors'
        'rights' of audience in Crown Courts. 35
Ford,; Husband of a Merry Wife of Windsor. 5
Foster, John QC
        A Recorder of Oxford and ladies' man, indicted
        for night poaching. 50

Gardens, Homes and, magazine,
        Former member of Md Ct indicted for allowing
        It to Visit and depict his Home and Garden 51
Gardiner, Gerald LC; Appoints BC 25
        Rebuked by H.Wilson for visiting RB 25
        Welcomes Courts Bill 35
Gerrard, Basil,
        Barrister on Nn Ct 18
GW's future wife's pupil- master 18
        Rebuked by HH Judge Nield, QC 18
Gibbens,Brian QC (later HH) 40*
        Appointed to Ct Bench 42
        Joint Leader of Md & Ox Ct 42
        Last Leader of Ox Ct 43
        Leads GW in R J-B C 85
        Obituary cited 43 Recorder of Oxford 39
        Shabbily treated by LC's Dept. 42
Gibbens,HH Terry; Appointed HH by mistake 42
Gifford, Lord QC; Opened chambers in Covent Garden 68
Gloucestershire; County on Ox Ct 14
        Last Assizes held at Gloucester. 37 note
        Lost to Wn Ct 45
Goff, Lord (Robert)
        J, LJ, and LAO 59note
Goodhart, Prof. Arnold,
        Guest of Ox Ct at dinner at University College 46
Goodman, Lord,
        Contended in House of Lords for solicitors' 'rights'
        Of audience and appointment in Crown Court 35

Hailsham, Douglas,LC
       Consulted AG and SG on eligibility of Oxford
       Circuiteers for Recordership of Birmingham 80
Hailsham, Quintin LC (son of Douglas)
       Introduced Cts Bill into House of Lords. 35
Halsbury, LC
       Appointed Darling QC to High Court Bench .58
Hamper, wicker; Used to transport Assize papers. 5
Hampshire,; A county on Wn Ct, nearly removed to S-E. 14, 45
Haydn, Joseph ; Composer of 'Oxford' Symphony. 1
Hell's Angels
       Slough Chapter routed at Pear Tree Roundabout 41 note
Hertfordshire,
       A county on Md Ct, formerly on Home Ct. 13
Holdsworth, Max
       A deputy/assistant Recorder at Oxford and
       Recorder of Lichfield 19
Home Circuit,
       A former Ct, comprising Essex, Kent, Sussex, Surrey
       And Hertfordshire 13
Homes and Gardens, see Gardens, Homes and
Hunt, Sir James, J.
       Abolished post of Deputy Leader of Md & Ox Ct 11
Hurd, Douglas, as Home Secretary appointed Stephen
       Tumim HM Chief Inspector of Prisons. 62
Hutton, Robert
       Distinguished an inference from a deduction 47
       Recorder of Reading and Chairman of Glos. QS 8

Imperial Chemical Industries,Ltd.
       RB's employers before/after Chairmanship of BC 25,37
       Did not appoint RB Chairman 37
Indictments, Ct, 48 seq
       Discontinued 50
Inner Temple, Honourable Society Of
       Acquired Serjeant's Inn, 69
       Awarded GW a scholarship 74
       Owned J.Andrews' map of Circuits 12
Irvine of Lairg, LC
       Appointed 121 new silks on 29th April

2003, but none thereafter 75
Irvine, James, (later HH); An 'accomplished gentleman' 63*
        His retirement dinner in Merton College. 63

Jenkins, Roy
        As Home Secretary, appointed BC in Nov. 1966 25.
Jones, Sir Kenneth,J (formerly HH) 59
Judge, the ambitious, since Beeching 68
Judicial Career Structure,since Beeching 67/8
Juke-Boxes,
        Subject-matter of fraud trial at Reading in 1964 84

Kent; A county on S-E (formerly on Home) Ct 13
King-Hamilton, Alan,QC (later HH) 82*
        A Leader of Ox Ct 89
        Appears in R J-B C 89 AppII
        Recalled GW's erstwhile looks 89
Kite Brief 78

Labour Government,
        Defeated in General Election in June 1970 35
Lancashire; A county on the Nn Ct 14
        South, a regional centre selected by BC 32
        Courts congested in 1950s 15 seq
Lane, Lord Chief Justice
        Intervened to keep Victorian Courts at Lincoln in use52
Laski, Neville QC
        Appointed Recorder of Liverpool (Crown Court) 18
        Not a successful appointment 18
Latham, Rt Hon Sir David, J. and LJ 59note
Lawson, Charles QC(later HH) 88
        Appeared in R J-B C 88
        Appointed Judge at Old Bailey 88
Leeds; A regional centre selected by BC 32
Leicester; A county on Md Ct 14
        Ancient Court in Castle 52
        Commented on by Prof. N. Pevsner, 52
        Very small judicial WC at. 52
Leviticus,; Cited by E.Terrell in Haley v LEB. 50
Lewis, William (Bill) T.D. 5

Last Ox Ct Clerk of Assize. 5
Lichfield; Max Holdsworth, Recorder of, 20
Lincoln; A county on Md Ct 14
        An Oxford College, where Ox Ct Ball held 46
        Victorian Courts saved by Lane LCJ. 52
Liverpool; Congestion in its Assizes and QS 15 seq
        Court of Passage, Harry Nelson its Judge 16
        Abolished by Courts Act 16
        Crown Court established in March 1956 17
        HH Judge Laski QC, its Recorder 18
London; Not on any Ct 13
        Old Bailey Assize Court for, 18
Lords Chancellor,
        Brougham 18
        Campbell 58
        Dilhorne 35
        Falconer 75
        Gardiner 25
        Hailsham,D. 80
        Hailsham,Q 35
        Irvine 45 note, 75
Lords Chief Justice
        Lane 52
        Parker 22 note, 35
        Woolf 60

Macclesfield, Lord; A lay magistrate at Oxon QS 8
MacKinnon, Sir Frank, J and LJ.
        Author of 'On Circuit', cited, 5
        His bicycle tyres pumped by future Lord Nuffield. 55
Maguire, Michael, QC; Leader of Nn Ct 42
        Refused to apply for 'new' Recordership 42
Manchester; Congestion at Assizes and QS. 15 seq
        Crown Court established in March 1956. 17
        HH Judge Nield QC its Recorder 18.
Marmalade; 'Oxford'. 1
Matthewman, Keith HH QC
        His opinions on modern Court design, cited. 53
May, Sir John, J. and LJ
        Declined, as Presiding Judge of the M&O Ct,

To approve appointment of any Circuit Judges. 61
Maxwell, Sir Alexander,
         Chairman of Committee on pressure at Assizes and
         QS in South Lancs. 16
Medd, Patrick QC; Last Recorder of Abingdon 47
Middlesex,; A county, including London, not on any Ct. 13
Middle Temple, Honourable Society of,
         Acquires premises in Essex Street. 69
         GW's wife a Bencher of, 69
Miller, Sir John, Master of the Horse
         Proprietor of Shotover Park, Headington, 56
         Provided lodgings for itinerant High Court Judges 56
Monmouthshire,; A county on Ox Ct, lost to W&C Ct. 14, 45
Morland, Sir Michael, J, and Nn Circuiteer, cited. 17
Morse, Det. Ch. Insptr.
         Investigated regrettably fictitious Oxford Murders 45
Murchie, John (later HH)An Ox Circuiteer and versifier. 86,87*
         Appeared at R J-B C. 86
         Convened 'survivors' dinner 44 note
Mynett, Kenneth QC (later HH) 41*
         Appeared for Crown at R J-B C 84
         Appointed to Circuit Bench 39*
         Frustrates sweep-stake at dinner in his honour. 41
         His hopes of further preferment dashed 39
         Wore 'silk's' gown after appointment as HH 39

National Archives at Kew.; Contained BC working papers 26
Nehru, Pandit, cited 37
Neill, Brian, J and LJ 59
Nelson, Henry Ince (Harry), QC; His career 15 seq
         His resignation from the Liverpool Recordership 17
         Its consequences 17
Newbury; Its QS abolished 48
         Its Recorder, Edward Terrell,QC 48
         His pretentions 48
Newport (Monmouthshire)
         An Ox Ct Assize town, lost to W&C Ct. 14
Nield, Basil QC MP
         A member of the Maxwell Committee, q.v. 18
         Appointed Recorder of Manchester, 18

Promoted to the High Court 18
Published account of Assize Towns 18
Rebuked GW's future wife's pupil master 18
Tried R J-B C 84
Norfolk; A county on S-E Ct 14
A former Ct 14
North-Eastern Ct; a division of former Nn Ct in 1876 14
Northern Ct; M.Maguire, QC,its leader 42
The western part of the former Nn Ct, after 1876. 14
Northumberland; A county on the N-E Circuit 14
Norwich Guildhall Court; Abolished by Cts Act
Nuffield, Lord
Inflated bicycle tyres of Frank MacKinnon 55

Oddie Christopher, (later HH); Appeared at R J-B C 84
Offa's Dyke,
Indignation West of, at BC plan to split W&C Ct 29
Old Bailey (Central Criminal Court)
Assize court for London Area, 18
Founded / extended by CCC Act 1834 17
Ox Ct Judges at
Alan King-Hamilton 89
Charles Lawson 88
BG 42
Orr, Alan, J and LJ 59
Oulton, Sir Derek; Secretary to BC 26
Unable to explain silence of BC on fate of Ox Ct 34 note
Oxford
Circuit
Abolished 45
Delineated 14
Merged with Md Ct 44
Colleges at,
Brasenose 46
Christ Church 46, 57
Keble 45 note
Lincoln 46
Pembroke 46 note
St John's 56
University 46

Courts in,
 Assize Court 53,54*
 Crown Court 55
 Magistrates' 55
 Town Hall 53
Streets of,
 Beaumont 66
 Blue Boar 21
 Folly Bridge 55
 High, The 88
 St Aldates' 55
 St Ebbe's 55
 St Giles' 56

Paddington; 8.05 from, to Oxford. 51
 Toast and boiled eggs eaten on 51
Paranoid Delusions; Suffered by GW 29 seq
Paull, Sir Gilbert
 GW, and others have painful lunch with 57
Pevsner, Sir Nikolaus, cited 52
Phillimore, J, later LJ, a member of BC 26
Pillow Cases, 'Oxford' 1
Polystyrene, expanded
 Royal Arms made of, in 'new' courts. 53
Popplewell, Sir Oliver J. 59

Quarter Sessions (QS)
 Abolished, 37
 Borough and County, 6
 Defects in system, 19 seq
 Described, 6 seq
Queen's Counsel (QC)
 Appointment of, Government antics on 75

Rawlinson, Sir Peter, QC
 AG in Edward Heath's Government, 35
 Introduced Courts Bill in House of Commons 36
Reading; R J-B C tried in second Court 84
 Removed to S-E Ct 44

Recorders
     Post-Courts Act 33
     Pre-Courts Act, 6
Rush, Michael
     Appeared at R J-B C 91
     Appointed HH 91
Rutland; A county on Md Ct 14

Sachs, Sir Eric J, and LJ. 59
Salford Hundred Court
     Abolished by Courts Act 37
     Discussed by BC 30
     Harry Nelson QC its Judge 16
Salop; A county on Ox Ct. 14
     QS deputy Chairmanship, a social desideratum 7
Saville, Mark, J, LJ and LAO 59
Sharp, Cartright, see Cartright Sharp
Sikes, William,'Prosecuted' for murder of Nancy 81
Simpson, Dean of Christ Church,
     Subjected with GW to Paull J's anecdotes 57
Slynn, Lord ; Appointed LAO direct from High Court 60
     His name dropped by KM 41
Soar, River,
     Worrying proximity to judicial WC at Leics Castle 52
Stafford,; An Ox Ct town 14
     GW has Kite brief at, 78
Stipendiary Magistrates; Defined 4
     Re-named District Judges 68
Streatfeild, Sir Geoffrey
     Chairman of Committee on reform or Assizes, etc 18,33.
Street, George Edmund,
     Architect of Royal Courts of Justice. 53
Stuart-White, Sir Christopher, J 59
Suffolk,Surrey and Sussex Counties on S-E Ct. 13

Talbot, Michael Chetwynd (later HH)
     Chairman of Salop QS 7
     Indicted by Ox Ct for Personation 50
     Junior for Crown at R J-B C 84
     Recorder of Banbury 47

Tedd Rex QC; Last Leader of Md & Ox Ct 45 note
          Resisted removal of Oxford to S-E Ct 45 note
Temple, Inner and Middle
          See Inner and Middle, supra
          Re-building since WWII 69.
Terrell, Edward, QC
          Appeared at R J-B C 90
          His book 49
          His character 48
          His entry in Who Was Who 48
          His inventions 49
          Indicted by Ox Ct for Blowing a Trumpet 49
          Recorder of Newbury 48
Tod, Mr.;Breaks into own house 3
          Finds Brock,T,q.v. there 3
          Has scalding tea thrown all over him 3
          Has violent fight with Brock,T supra 3
Trollope, Anthony
          County magistrates at QS a survival from8
Trousers; 'Oxford Bags' 1
Tucker, Sir Richard, J 59
          An eloquent advocate on Circuit Indictments 49
Tumim, Stephen (later HH and Sir)
          A Castaway on Desert Island Discs 62
          An 'accomplished gentleman' 61*
          Appointed to Circuit Bench 62
          Appointed H.M.Chief Inspector of Prisons 62
          Threatened by I.R.A. 62

Underhill, Michael QC (later HH)
          The best advocate on Circuit Indictments. 49

Verdi, Guiseppi,; Composer of 'Falstaff' 5

Wales: Circuits, Four/Two 13/14
          Prince of,
              Remarried in Windsor Guildhall 21
          & Chester Circuit 12
              Abolition nearly proposed by BC 29
              Reprieved. 29

Wanda, a Fish Called
 Cleese, J.q.v. appeared in GW's place in, 3
Weitzman, Peter QC; An Ox Ct leader of Md & Ox Ct 44
White, Frank (later HH and Sir)
 An 'accomplished gentleman'. 63
 Snr Circuit Judge at Central London County Court 64
 Summer Party for CLCC, instituted by 64
Wilson, Harold, HH
 A Senior Circuit Judge at Oxford. vii
 A valuable Consultant vii
Winchester; Nearly removed to S-E Ct 45 note
Windsor; Guildhall used as Court by QS 20
 Musical interruptions at 20
 Prince of Wales remarried at 21
 Merry Wives of, 5
  Their hamper 5
Wrightson, Paul QC; Appeared at R J-B C 85
Wood, John, Sir, J. 59
Woolf, Lord (Harry); his brilliant career 60

Yorkshire; A county on N-E, formerly on Nn, Ct 14